JESUIT
SPIRITUALITY

JESUIT SPIRITUALITY

A NOW AND FUTURE RESOURCE

JOHN W. O'MALLEY, SJ • JOHN W. PADBERG, SJ • VINCENT T. O'KEEFE, SJ

A Campion Book

Loyola University Press
Chicago

∞

Loyola University Press
3441 North Ashland Avenue
Chicago, Illinois 60657

The addresses and responses contained in this book were pre-sented at the Ignatian Charism Days held in June of 1989 at Loyola University of Chicago by the Chicago Province of the Society of Jesus.

Library of Congress Cataloging-in-Publication Data

Jesuit spirituality : a now and future resource / John W. O'Malley, John W. Padberg, Vincent T. O'Keefe.
    p.   cm. — (A Campion book)
    Contents : Some distinctive characteristics of Jesuit spiri-tuality in the sixteenth century / John W. O'Malley — Predict-ing the past, looking back for the future / John W. Padberg — Jesuit Spirituality / Vincent T. O'Keefe — Responses / Wilton D. Gregory, Carol Frances Jegen.
    ISBN 0-8294-0699-9
    1. Jesuits—Spiritual life. 2. Jesuits—Theology. 3. Spiritu-ality—Catholic Church. 4. Catholic Church—Doctrines—His-tory. I. O'Malley, John W. II. Padberg, John W. III. O'Keefe, Vincent T.
BX3703.J42 1990
248'.08'822—dc20   90-39457
                                                                CIP

Ad majorem Dei gloriam

Contents

Foreword

Following the Chicago Province Congregation in January, 1987, I asked the delegates to discuss areas of our Jesuit life that required attention. While we have been able to evaluate and plan for ministry effectively, the delegates expressed concern about our inner life: our ability to pray together, our appropriation of our spiritual heritage, our confidence in Ignatian spirituality, our willingness to support one another.

In response to these concerns, I convened a group of eight Jesuits in May, 1987, and asked them whether the Chicago Province should undertake any common, province-wide effort in the area of spirituality. If so, what would they recommend to enable our men to appropriate our Ignatian spirituality at a deeper level? And finally, what would they recommend we do to facilitate communicating our spirituality to our collaborators and to the people to whom we minister? Armed with these questions, the group, which became known as the "Spirituality Committee," worked out a detailed set of recommendations.

The committee canvassed the Jesuit communities of the province twice. They learned that there was a strong interest in the spiritual renewal of the province. Province members wanted the opportunity to appropriate more deeply our Ignatian charism. The committee recommended that each province member attend to personal prayer in some form of companionship with other members of the province, that the "19th Annotation Ignatian retreat" be highly encouraged for all, beginning in the fall of 1988, as well as community dialogs and exhortations on Ignatian spirituality; that there should be province-wide days of learning and reflection on the Ignatian Charism in June of 1989; and that in June of 1990 there should be an "Ignatian Charism Retreat." I am happy to report that we were able to follow up on all of the committee's recommendations.

The presentations and the comments offered at the June, 1989, Ignatian Charism days are gathered here as *Jesuit Spirituality*. The presentation of Father John W. O'Malley, S.J., was given on the morning of June 10, that of Father John W. Padberg, S.J., on the afternoon of the same day. Following each of their presentations there was an opportunity to raise questions and to participate in discussion groups. On the morning of June 11, Father Vincent T. O'Keefe, S.J., offered his reflections, which were followed by the responses of Bishop Wilton D. Gregory and Sister Carol Frances Jegen, B.V.M.

It was not planned originally that these presentations be gathered as a book. The response of those who attended the Charism days, however, became a groundswell pressing for publication.

Nothing remains but to thank all who participated in the Charism days. The excellent contents of the presentations speak for themselves. The generosity of the speakers taught us, by example, how we might more effectively appropriate our Ignatian heritage.

Robert A. Wild, S.J.
Provincial of the Chicago Province
May 15, 1990

1

Some Distinctive Characteristics of Jesuit Spirituality in the Sixteenth Century

John W. O'Malley, S.J.

We often hear that Saint Ignatius and his companions were attuned to their times, and that that is the reason for the growth that the Society of Jesus attained in comparison with similar groups like the Barnabites and the Theatines founded just a few years earlier. When we examine the Society against other spiritualities current in the sixteenth century, what first strikes us, in fact, is the many points that it had in common with them, even appropriated from them, as I hope to show. What were the reasons, then, that almost immediately propelled the spirituality of the Society on a course that was distinctive and, for the most part, more widely received?

We must first of all take account of certain factors that were extrinsic to Jesuit spirituality, and only then can we leave them behind. I mean things like the international character and experience of the original seven companions—Iberians, by and large, who studied in Paris and then settled with Rome as their headquarters. I mean the degrees from the University of Paris that they all held and which gave them a status of which they were proud. I mean the fact that their leader, Saint Ignatius, lived for almost a generation after the Society was founded and was able to give it direction during those crucial years. I mean the mix of social classes represented by the original band. I mean the entré that Ignatius' social position gave him to members of the house of Hapsburg, related by marriage to the pope, Paul III, who first approved the Society in 1540.

These were important factors in the beginning, but they do not get to the heart of the matter. The Jesuits had something more intrinsic, something distinctive, as my title indicates, that accounts for their success. Difficult though it is to do so in such a complex matter, I shall try to put my finger on some characteristics of that distinctiveness. It will come as no surprise that the first and most basic source and symbol of Jesuit distinctiveness was a book, the *Spiritual Exercises*. The *Exercises* was not only a book that contained spiritual teaching, but it also contained in embryo the basic design for Jesuit spirituality and ministry. Although there were some vague earlier precedents, the *Exercises* founded one of Catholicism's most fundamental instruments of ministry, the retreat. That in itself was no mean accomplishment, but the importance of the *Exercises* reaches much further.

Before I elaborate on that matter, however, I must insist that Jesuit spirituality in the sixteenth century cannot be reduced to the *Exercises*, even though grounded in them. It was also expressed in the vast quantity of writings that the first Jesuits produced—first of all the seemingly limitless amount of their correspondence (the extant correspondence of Ignatius alone exceeds that of any other sixteenth-century figure), the Constitutions and Ignatius' so-called *Autobiography*, the many exhortations and other documents for internal consumption produced by Jerónimo Nadal, the memoranda, chronicles, and pastoral aids of Juan de Polanco, the works on piety and ministry by more obscure figures like Gaspar Loarte and Cristóforo de Madrid, the catechisms by Canisius, and other works by other authors.

The fact that very little of this literature was published until almost four centuries after the death of the authors accounts for the sometimes confused, sometimes erroneous, ideas we have inherited about the early spirituality of the Society. Moreover, unless one is, like myself, addicted to such materials, most of it is not exactly scintillating reading. This explains why most of what has been written in recent years about Jesuit spirituality is based almost exclusively on the *Exercises,* with an occasional sideways glance at the Constitutions.

The almost overwhelming mass of this documentation discourages all but the most intrepid and makes it difficult to discover a coherent pattern. I let myself be guided by certain words or phrases that recur so insistently as to indicate something of great concern. We are used to the idea, for instance, that "the greater glory of God" is one of these. Since it is so familiar, I will not dwell on it but call your attention to three others that are less grandiloquent but perhaps even more prevalent. They are, in order of ascending frequency, "our way of proceeding," "consolation," and "helping souls."

Each of these terms, like the *Exercises* themselves, are condensed symbols of elements central to Jesuit spirituality in the sixteenth century. It would be only a slight exaggeration to state that the last two occur explicitly or implicitly on almost every page of the early documents. Just the listing of the three of them together suggests the intimate and intrinsic relationship, absolutely basic, between Jesuit spirituality and the practice of ministry.

We perhaps get our best idea of what these terms encapsulate by first looking at other spiritualities that were prevalent in the sixteenth century, indicating actual or possible influences on the first Jesuits or, when that is not possible, parallels and divergences, and then, finally, returning to the particular synthesis or mix that the early Jesuits created. The danger in such a procedure is that we might seem to discount the most important factor of all, the religious experience of Ignatius himself. One cannot insist enough that that experience is the touchstone for all subsequent Jesuit spirituality, codified in a demysticized way in the *Exercises.*

Let it be said once and for all: the respect Ignatius had for his own experience imparted to him respect for the religious experience of others. In some ways, it seems to me, this is the hallmark of Jesuit spirituality and ministry. Nonetheless, Ignatius' experience was filtered to him through the categories that his age and culture offered him and was further articulated through the spiritual and pastoral instruments that were at hand that provided elements out of which to construct a new synthesis. Without any doubt the *Devotio Moderna* was the movement that in general and particular had the most influence on Ignatius and the first companions. Perhaps better said, that is the influence that can be most clearly and specifically identified. As we know, that amorphous movement began in the Low Countries in the late fourteenth century, flourished there in the fifteenth, and from there it had spread by the beginning of the sixteenth to certain devout circles elsewhere in Europe. Ignatius first encountered it in a significant way with the Benedictine monks of Montserrat and at the same time or shortly thereafter at Manresa in the most widely circulated document of the movement, the *Imitation of Christ*. Whether he and his companions realized it or not, they further encountered it at the University of Paris in the discipline of the Collège de Montaigu, where Ignatius first studied, and even in the so-called *modus parisiensis*, that peculiar blend of content and pedagogical methods that the Jesuits adopted and adapted for their educational enterprise. The *modus parisiensis*, despite what the term implies, fundamentally originated not in Paris but in the Low Countries with the *Devotio*. (Those early Jesuits who had already studied at Alcalá would have encountered the *modus parisiensis* there as well.)

We know for certain one thing that Ignatius learned at Montserrat—the general confession of devotion, i.e., that moral inventory that does not look so much to absolution from sin, which presumably has been accomplished in other confessions, as to deeper sorrow so as to begin a new way of life. The origins of this devout exercise are extemely obscure. It probably originated in the late fifteenth century with the *Devotio*, to which Abbot Cisneros was deeply indebted for his reform of the monastery of Montserrat just a short while before Ignatius' arrival there. The Abbot obliged the novices to spend almost two weeks preparing for that confession before they made their profession. Ignatius, guest of the monastery in 1522, did a modified version of it in three days. At present we know of no other place besides Montserrat where it was practiced.

Ignatius and the first Jesuits popularized the idea, and,

as we know, it is the culmination of the first conversion that the *Exercises* envision before they move onto the further conversion prompted by the Second Week and confirmed by the last two. Conversion of heart was, of course, not exactly a new idea in Christianity. What the general confession did, however, was to provide a mode in which it could be articulated, ritualized, and blessed. It gave it a "way of proceeding."

In their ministry and spirituality the first Jesuits were mad with the graces that the sacrament of Penance offered, but they almost inevitably became entangled in the juridical and casuistical morass of late-medieval speculation about it. Some few scholars today are beginning to recognize the positive side of medieval and Counter-Reformation casuistry. There can be no doubt, however, that the juridical model underlying much speculation about the sacrament could engender in both confessor and penitent the anxiety and guilt that the sacrament was, in fact, supposed to relieve and could blunt or destroy the consolation that the Jesuits (and others) insisted was the principal fruit of the sacrament.

Under normal circumstances the general confession bypassed those speculations and let both confessor and penitent deal more freely with the movements of the heart, with consolations and desolations. Its important place in early Jesuit ministry gives us insight into the kind of conversion and the mode of sealing it that was the foundation of their spirituality for themselves and others. It is significant that the first book on the spiritual life written by a Jesuit, Gaspar Loarte's *Esercitio della vita spirituale,* published in 1557, begins with a chapter on this kind of general confession. The book was intended not for the elite but for lowly folk, even for the illiterate, to whom, Loarte suggests, it could be read by a more fortunate neighbor.

Probably at Montserrat, surely from the *Imitation* at Manresa, Ignatius learned the benefits of frequent communion. Frequent communion had been proposed by leading theologians like Jean Gerson in the early fifteenth century. To say the least, it had not caught on even in most convents and monasteries, where generally five or six times a year was considered a safe norm. Reception of communion as often as once a week or more became distinctive of Jesuit spirituality and ministry, for which they suffered, as we all know, a great deal of grief from the very earliest days. Others at about the same time were taking up the cause, but none with such insistence and notoriety as the Jesuits.

The Jesuits for the most part had nothing new to say about the benefits to be derived from receiving the Eucharist. If you want to know what they thought, read the pertinent chapters from the fourth book of the *Imitation*. Their distinctiveness lay, rather, in two other areas. First, they insisted that these benefits be frequently received as nourishment for one's ongoing spiritual pilgrimage. That is obvious.

The second is more subtle but perhaps more important. In order to promote frequent communion, they had to overcome the "worthiness-unworthiness" arguments that medieval spirituality and theology had produced concerning reception of the Eucharist. It is not too much to say that these arguments at least flirted with Pelagianism and Semi-Pelagianism and also with some curious views, in particular, about human sexuality. As you know, some theologians proposed that even married persons could not receive the Eucharist if they had had intercourse the night, or even the week, before.

The basic Jesuit response to the unworthiness line was simplicity itself: you come to the Eucharist not because you are sated but because you are hungry, not because you are warm but because you are cold, not because you are worthy (no one is) but because you are unworthy. We are familiar today with such reasoning. What we must remember about it, especially in the context of the sixteenth century, is its anti-Pelagian core.

The first Jesuits were restrained in speaking about sexual issues. By and large they seem to have accepted the received wisdom on it, but at least one of them strove to dispell some taboos. I must quote for you an outspoken passage from the outspoken Nicolas Bobadilla, 1551: "Some theologians give another reason for abstaining from the Eucharist, that is, nocturnal pollution—about which they philosophize with a thousand distinctions. Well, my opinion is that neither noctural nor diurnal pollution, neither while asleep nor while awake, neither in legitimate matrimony nor in lust outside it, neither anything mortally sinful nor venially is an obstacle to communion, provided the person has repented any sin and confessed it. Forgiveness for sin does not, indeed, happen over a period of time but is instantaneous."

In that same work, a broadside against worthiness doctrines, Bobadilla insists on the right of the faithful to receive communion as often as they want. He was specifically asked if a pastor might legitimately refuse communion to lay persons who wanted to receive *daily*. For the sixteenth century, and perhaps even more for our own, his response was daring. Nobody—no pastor, no bishop, no pope could deprive the faithful of the "liberty to communicate"—*libertatem communicandi*. As you can see, the issue of frequent communion had ramifications for spirituality that might at first escape us. The "freedom of the Christian" was Luther's special theme, but the Jesuits too had a version of it.

The *Devotio Moderna* also provided the elements for the methods of "contemplation" and application of the senses that we find in the *Exercises*, and it promoted daily examination of conscience. Thus we see that it promoted method or procedure in the spiritual life, descending to concrete details of "how-to." If we view it large, moreover, it had other elements that correlate with early Jesuit spirituality, even if we cannot be certain about the degree of direct impact. Although the *Devotio* emphasized external discipline and tended to an arid and almost stoic moralism at times, as did some of the Jesuits, it more basically tried to foster what is known as "inwardness." That often meant valuing the movements of the heart over the thoughts of the head. God speaking within was the center, which of course resonated with Ignatius' experience while he recuperated at Loyola and while he led a hermit's life at Manresa.

What did the *Devotio* lack that the Jesuits had? First of all, that fundamental commitment to "helping souls." The spirituality of the *Devotio* was to that extent self-enclosed, a mere variation of the fundamental themes of monastic spirituality. Therefore, although it fostered method, it never applied it in a consistent way to ministry. It was basically elitist, for even the *Imitation* postulates the conditions of the cloister for the silence and recollection it commends. It lacked a clear articulation of the basic design of the spiritual life that the *Exercises* at least implicitly contains and which the first Jesuits saw when they intepreted the design as the traditional path from purification to enlightenment to union—"the three ways."

Although the *Devotio* was not really anti-intellectual, despite accusations against it to that effect, it was anti-scholastic in some of its authors. It offered, however, no clear alternatives to scholastic theology. It lacked, therefore, especially in the *Imitation*, a firm theological base that would save it from the pitfalls of its moralism, of a monastic and stoic "contempt of the world," of a pervasive "worthiness" doctrine, even of subtle or blatant Pelagianism or Semi-Pelagianism.

That brings us to the intellectual and theological experience of the companions at the University of Paris. It is astounding how little—practically nothing—Ignatius has to say about it in the *Autobiography*. The others tell us little more. They were there, moreover, when the University was not in one of its better periods. They had a basically eclectic education, and they spent most of their time not on theology but on "philosophy" in the Arts faculty—learning a curious mixture of Aristotelian science and medieval logic and dialectics. The university had, nonetheless, great influence on them, for they thereafter expressed themselves most facilely in formal situations in scholastic patterns of argument—although, for different reasons, that generalization applies less to Ignatius and Nadal than to the rest of them.

Did it have an impact in any other ways? I will mention two. The first is certain, the second conjectural. There is no doubt that, proud as they were of their alma mater, even after the condemnation of the Society by the theological faculty of Paris in 1554, they either in practice forswore or in theory explicitly repudiated the purely academic bias with which theology was taught at Paris. That might come as somewhat of a surprise to you, but it was already suggested in the passage earlier quoted from Bobadilla. Nadal was at times even fiercer and more forthright.

Limitations of time force me to reduce their criticism to

the bare bones of saying that the theologians of Paris lived in their heads, not their hearts, and they practiced their discipline for the sake of their colleagues not for the Lord's flock. In other words, they divorced theology from both spirituality and from the practice of ministry. Others had earlier pointed out these two divorces, for the *Devotio* had implicitly given voice to the first, and Erasmus and other humanists explicitly to both. They had all as a result repudiated scholastic theology, whereas the Jesuits hoped to reshape it, at least for themselves.

Nadal in a famous passage from an exhortation at Alcalá in 1561 referred to Ignatius as "our father, the theologian." He probably does not lack here some polemical intent, for the condemnation of the Society had not been retracted and the sting of Melchior Cano's rabid attacks was still being felt. In context it is clear in any case that this is a theologian in a new key, a theologian who relates study to ministry, without which study made no sense for members of the Society.

In the eleventh of the Rules for Thinking with the Church, Ignatius commends both the "positive doctors" (i.e., the Fathers of the Church) and the "scholastics" [363]. While in further Jesuit documentation from this early period one hears more about Aristotle and Aquinas, the positive doctors supplied part of the corrective to the scholastics that the Jesuits thought was needed—as that rule states, the power "to rouse the affections, so that we are moved to love and serve God our Lord in all things." The Jesuits stood for a learned ministry and, to that degree, a learned spirituality. But it was a learning that had to conform to "our way of proceeding."

The second way that the University of Paris had an impact is, as I said, conjectural, at least for Ignatius. As far as I know, H. Outram Evennett was the first to suggest it in his little classic, *The Spirit of the Counter-Reformation.* Evennett believed that at Paris Ignatius found, especially in Saint Thomas, the intellectual and theological basis for his reconciliation with the world that had begun at Manresa when he surrendered his excessive mortifications. This makes sense, for the Ignatian documents beyond the *Exercises* breathe even more clearly the conviction that grace builds on nature. Among the scholastics Aquinas was in the forefront in basing his system on that principle, and he is, of course, specified in the Constitutions as the theological authority for the order [464].

Polanco surely studied Aquinas at the University of Padua and seems to have grasped the essentials of his system. Perhaps to Polanco as much as to Ignatius we owe the firm weaving into the fabric of the *Constitutions* the principle that grace and nature somehow correlate. In the many writings of Nadal, however, we find the most explicit and unswerving adherence to the idea that nature and grace are reconciliable, along with insistence on the preeminence and prevenient character of the latter that saved the system within a Catholic framework from Pelagianism and Semi-Pelagianism. He is the person who in his exhortations to practically every Jesuit community in Europe taught the Society its spirituality and provided explicit theological undergirdings for it, basically a theology of reconciliation and of a world "charged with the grandeur of God."

I fear that not all the early Jesuits avoided the pitfalls of the Semi-Pelagianism of which they have been so often accused. Some passages of Polanco are at best ambigious, as are some even of Ignatius. With the latter, however, the *"Suscipe"* prayer, as the final culmination of Ignatian spirituality, provides the best key to interpreting him [234]. In that prayer there is no question of saving or sanctifying oneself but of total submission to the movements of grace.

Somewhere, moreover, Nadal picked up the idea that there was lots of grace around. This allowed him a "Christian optimism" about spirituality and ministry that was surely not found in everybody in the often dour sixteenth century. To be anti-Pelagian *and* optimistic—that was his feat, for which he was indebted in large part to Aquinas and Bonaventure.

Although Nadal was faithful to the teaching of the Third Week and saw in Jesuits men "who were crucified to the world," he and others were able to give this teaching an interpretation that saved it from world-hate and led them to "find God in all things" (*Const.* 288). It further led Nadal to his astounding statement about members of the Society, repeated by him often in his exhortations: "The world is our house" or "The world is our home."

The corollary of this statement is that Jesuit ministry, and, hence, Jesuit spirituality, is intended for every category of person in the world, no matter what their spiritual or religious situation, no matter what their "state in life." Only those in special need have special claim. Otherwise it is about as non-elitist and non-discriminatory as one can imagine. With the first Jesuits this was not only their theory but their invariable practice, no matter what course the future history of the Society took. As the Jesuits were ministers themselves, they tried to engage others to help them and to continue ministries they had begun. This is graphically illustrated in their training of lay catechists, even young boys, and in the many confraternities they founded long before the "Marian Congregation" or Sodality was founded at the Roman College in 1563.

Although some of the first Jesuits would have met and begun to appropriate elements of Renaissance Humanism at Alcalá, they were more deeply exposed to it at Paris. From the very beginning and at the core of the humanist movement was spiritual and moral reform, even though these features might at times have become obscured. The movement eventually developed a rather coherent spirituality that achieved its apex in the writings of Erasmus. For centuries that aspect of Erasmus was scorned rather than studied, and only in the past two decades have we begun to discover the depths of his spirituality—and, I might add, its many similarities with the spirituality of the first Jesuits, unaware though most Jesuits seem to have been of these similarities.

Erasmus, too, sought a more inward spirituality—based on the Bible and the Fathers. He objected to the aridity of much of the theological speculation of his day, and therefore tried to reconcile theology with piety through recourse to the patristic tradition. He hoped, in fact, to give contours to a spirituality appropriate for persons living outside the cloister, especially married women and men. In his many writings he tried not only to jettison some of the claptrap and mechanical techniques of the pastoral practices of his day but also to provide an alternative ideal that, as I said, in some particulars resembles the Jesuits'.

My hunch is that he had more influence, at least indirect,

on the early Jesuits than we have been led to believe. Polanco, for instance, studied Erasmus' ground-breaking treatise on preaching while he was at the University of Padua. Nonetheless, the first Jesuits, including Ignatius, became cautious about him, although the degree of their caution has been exaggerated by Jesuit historians, and the reasons for it sometimes distorted. They, in any case, disliked the sarcasm of his criticism of pious practices and were wary of his historico-critical approach to the texts of the Bible and the Fathers. Their failure to appreciate the historico-critical aspect of the humanist movement had, in my opinion, some truly unhappy results.

Nonetheless, for all the good things that can be said about Erasmus' writings on spirituality and ministry, they are deficient in comparison with the Jesuits in at least one important regard: they lack the detail of how-to. Erasmus wrote beautifully on prayer, but even his treatise entitled "How to Pray to God" does not exactly tell you how to do it in the concrete ways the *Exercises* does. The same deficiency can be found in his treatises related to ministry, even the treatise on preaching. In that he differed immensely from the Jesuits as well as from certain aspects of the *Devotio Moderna*.

One thing all the Jesuits learned at Paris from the humanist tradition in general, Nadal better than the others, was to speak and write Latin in a humanist style. In one way that is an altogether superficial appropriation of the humanist tradition, but in other ways most profound. Changes in style, after all, imply changes in *forma mentis*. The style is the man, and all that.

The humanists believed that their style of discourse allowed them the best entrance into their interlocutor's humanity and deepest aspirations. Freed of professional jargon, it facilitated meaningful converse with anybody on the major questions about human life and destiny. That, of course, was the ideal, for not too deep under the surface was a good dose of snobbishness, which, however, could be left behind by those who wished to.

The early Jesuits assiduously cultivated "spiritual conversation." An ancient tradition that, but the humanists also cultivated conversation as part of their opposition to dialectical debate, and Erasmus left behind a sublime example of "spiritual conversation" in his colloquy entitled "The Godly Feast." Jesuit spiritual conversation correlated with this development. Nadal, who tells us most about it among the early Jesuits, himself composed two long "dialogues" or "colloquies," which, if not directly modeled on Erasmus himself, certainly are modeled on those of lesser known humanists.

The humanists' style was, of course, related to their cultivation of rhetoric, the art of speaking and writing persuasively. The Jesuits eagerly seized this aspect of the humanist tradition. What does that have to do with ministry and spirituality? Just about everything. Rhetoric, in the basic sense, is the art of public speaking, and public speaking is successful to the extent that the speaker is in touch with the feelings of the audience. It is to them that he accommodates what he has to say.

When the Jesuits tried to "help souls," they were admonished again and again to do so in a way that took account of time, place, and circumstance and especially the spiritual condition of those to whom they ministered. Ignatius and the first Jesuits did not discover this idea for the first time in the humanist tradition, but that tradition gave them further grounding for it and classic articulation. It was a key element in their "way of proceeding." In other words, despite all the rules, annotations, and suggestions in the *Exercises*, the cardinal principle was accommodation to the person making them. Basic to "our way of proceeding" was that, within limits, you could throw it out if it did not seem to be working.

As the art of *public* speaking, rhetoric looked to public lives, to life in the world. The spirituality developed by some of the humanists in Renaissance Rome had precisely this dimension to it; it was intended for persons outside the cloister. I suggest that the more intense cultivation of rhetoric by the second generation of Jesuits helped confirm the outside-the-cloister aspect of Jesuit spirituality that was present in the life of Ignatius the pilgrim from the beginning.

Ah, the cloister! One of the most powerful spiritual movements of the fifteenth century was the so-called observantist reforms among the older religious orders, of which the reform of Carmel by Teresa and John of the Cross would be sixteenth-century manifestations. The basic idea was that the spiritual objectives of religious life would be best secured by an exact observance of the Rule and its authentic customaries down to the last detail.

As is obvious, Jesuit spirituality for members of the Society could not in the beginning subscribe to such a spirituality, for they had no Rule to observe besides the papal bulls of 1540 and 1550 until the Constitutions were known and promulgated—which was not done officially until after the death of Ignatius. Moreover, the well known attitude of Ignatius and the companions towards choir indicates that at least at the beginning they were far removed from an "observantist" mentality. It was not in the observance of the Rule, as that expression was generally understood, that spiritual perfection lay, but in living out according to God's will the call to "help souls" heard in the meditations on the Kingdom and the Two Standards.

Even during Ignatius' lifetime, however, rules began to multiply in the Society, and Nadal, my hero, produced them at a great rate. They functioned at first principally as what we would today call "job-descriptions," and were desperately needed. But one already begins to detect a shift in perspective about how "perfection" was achieved toward exact observance of "the rules." The observantist movement had its impact, and the generalates of Francisco Borgia and Everard Mercurian seem to have provided it with more support than it had under Ignatius and Lainez.

Nonetheless, a wider vision also operated, made possible to some extent by the new rhetoric, which by definition liked to look to big issues. Nadal became skilled in that rhetoric and was thus able to articulate Jesuit spirituality with a force and vision that even Ignatius could not muster. This led him to speak about Jesuit spirituality, first of all for Jesuits themselves and then for others, in ways that defied the idea that perfection lay in the cloister. Let me quote again a passage I called to your attention in an issue of *Studies*. Nadal has been speaking about the three types of houses (or "cloisters") mentioned in the *Constitutions*—novitiates, colleges, professed houses. Then he adds his own—the journeys, pilgrimages, or "missions," as they are called in the fourth vow. He calls the journey our "fourth kind of house."

> That [fourth house] is altogether the most ample place and reaches as far as the globe itself. For wherever they can be sent in ministry to help souls, that is the most glorious and longed-for "house" for those theologians. For they know the goal set before them: to procure the salvation and perfection of all women and men. They understand that they are to that end bound by that fourth vow to the supreme pontiff: that they are to go on these universal journeys for the help of souls by his command, which by divine decree extends throughout the whole Church. They realize that they cannot build or acquire enough houses to be able from nearby to run out to the combat. Since that is the case, they consider that they are in their most peaceful and pleasant house when they are constantly on the move, when they travel throughout the earth, when they have no place to call their own, when they are always in need, always in want—only let them strive in some small way to imitate Christ Jesus, who had nowhere on which to lay his head and who spent all his years of preaching in journey.

Two models underlie the vision of the pastoral spirituality of the Society, as the above citation suggests: the itinerant preaching of Jesus and his disciples and the evangelizing journeys of Paul. About the latter Nadal says explicitly: *Paul* is our model for ministry. Paul, the theologian of the gratuity of grace, was central to Luther's spirituality. He meant the same for Nadal, but he and other early Jesuits further insisted on the Pauline mystical identification with Christ and especially on Paul the tireless evangelizer. That last was particularly muted in Luther.

This romp through sixteenth-century spiritualities that I have been leading might leave you with the impression that what was distinctive of Jesuit spirituality was that it adopted and adapted all that was best in the age and left the dross behind. That would be nonsense, of course. If we did not know it already, we need read only a few sources to realize that the early Jesuits were just human beings—energetic, committed, agile of mind, intensely devout, willing to learn from their mistakes—but, like us, creatures of their own time and place. We do them and ourselves a disservice if we invest them with an omniscience and inerrancy they did not possess. I have not here dwelt on their sixteenth-century limitations but on elements that transcend them and have positive application for today.

Despite their limitations, the achievements of the first Jesuits were astounding. Among them was the forging of a distinctive spirituality. The *Magna Carta* of that spirituality was unquestionably the *Exercises*. In order to fully understand Jesuit spirituality in the sixteenth century, however, we cannot rest satisfied simply with the text of the *Exercises*, for we must go beyond it to see how the Jesuits, including Ignatius himself, elaborated from it and interpreted it, to compare it with other spiritualities, to set it in its historical context.

Having attempted to sketch that context, even in such a rapid and superficial way, let me just list some of the factors that, *taken together* as part of a mix or synthesis, contributed to a distinctive spirituality:

1. The early Jesuits had a *book*, recognized by all as the normative and quintessential expression of what they were ultimately about—conversion of heart from sin and then conversion to discipleship in poverty and service. In Roman Catholicism in the sixteenth century, no other group had such a document, such a clear focus.

2. The early Jesuits inculcated a number of devout practices—frequent confession and communion, daily examination of conscience, regular spiritual direction, and so forth. Not these but conversion of heart from sin and conversion to discipleship were, however, the center of their spirituality. Devout practices were to be employed in the way and to the degree they sustained and advanced conversion.

3. In the *Exercises* the Jesuits found a general design for the spiritual journey, which they articulated in classic terms as a movement from purgation to enlightenment to union of their wills with the divine will. This was their ultimate design for their *ministry* as well as their lives. Their spirituality did not,

therefore, consist in a program of practices that assumed the spiritual life was static or circular.

4. In the *Exercises* they found, as well, an agreed-upon criterion for judging the authenticity of every step of the journey—consolation. While the movements of the good and evil spirits cannot, of course, be reduced to emotions or feelings, they are in the first instance registered there. Thus the early Jesuits paid much attention to dispositions of the heart in the making of choices, to the dismay of persons like Melchior Cano, who attacked them on this ground.

5. The wayfarer was not to be left without directives, so they elaborated, as did the *Exercises*, practical suggestions down to minute detail according to which he or she might proceed. They themselves had a number of "ways of proceeding" that they considered peculiarly their own.

6. Nonetheless, accommodation to the concrete circumstances of the individual was the principle underlying all the "ways of proceeding." This lent their spirituality and ministry a decidedly "rhetorical" character. Just as the orator must be in touch with the feelings and expectations of his audience, so must the minister be in touch with the needs, problems, and aspirations of those unto whom he ministers. Thus Jesuit spirituality and ministry evince a certain flexibility.

7. Since their spirituality could be accommodated to persons in all conditions and states of life, it could be applied both inside and outside the cloister. For themselves, the most dramatic expression of this feature of their spirituality was the fourth vow pronounced by the professed but seen as an ideal for all. "The world is our house."

8. Applicable to all states of life, their spirituality implicitly recognized the validity of all vocations. The elections in the *Exercises* were to be done in "Christian liberty." The Jesuits were, in fact, heavily criticized because they taught "indifference" even regarding the life of the three vows.

9. Although their way of expressing themselves opened them and those unto whom they ministered to the dangers of a stoical and even Semi-Pelagian interpretation of the spiritual life, their best and more fundamental statements insisted on the primacy of grace and the necessity of utter commitment of

oneself to its movements.

10. The underlying Thomistic framework of the Constitutions, the exhortations of Nadal, and other primary documents at least implied that nature and grace, while somehow discontinuous with each other, were also reconciliable. This provided the Jesuits' religious vision with more optimism about the world and human nature than we find in many other movements of the sixteenth century. Their spirituality assumed an engagement with culture, not withdrawal from it.

11. Their starting point, as is perlucidly clear from Ignatius' *Autobiography*, was the desire to "help souls." They interpreted this term broadly to mean souls and *bodies*, and, hence, their commitment to the corporal works of mercy as well as to every form of spiritual ministry. As de Guibert said so well years ago, "service" is at the core of Jesuit spirituality.

12. Theirs was, then, a pastoral or ministerial spirituality. To understand it we must look as much to the history of ministry as we do to the history of spirituality—faltering though our efforts have been along this line up to the present. Their synonym for "helping souls" was ministry—*ministerium, ministeria*, words preeminently proper to the Society of Jesus and not "borrowed from Protestants," as we sometimes hear tell.

I will conclude by returning to the three terms I mentioned at the beginning. First, "our way of proceeding." The first Jesuits used this expression to mean many things, referring it most obviously to the primary documents of the Society—the papal bulls of approbation and confirmation, the *Constitutions*, the *General Examen*, etc. They also referred it to the various rules, customs, ways of governing and behaving. More generally, it meant a certain *style*—simple, direct, unpretentious, unostentatious, unforbidding—*familiaris* is the word they often used to capture it. It meant for Jesuit ministry and spirituality that it descended to specific details of "how-to."

"Our way of proceeding" was geared to "helping souls" and bodies—helping souls and bodies as they here and now are, not as they ought to be according to somebody's ideal. This meant that the details of "our way of proceeding" had to yield to the ultimate principle of accommodation to the needs of the people in front of them—and often enough this meant the unchurched, the outcast, the unbeliever. Central to "our way of proceeding to help souls" was to go out to persons in such need, on long and painful journeys if necessary, not to wait at the doorsteps of the first three kinds of houses. (I do not recall them ever saying they were "saving" souls—the modesty implicit in simply "helping" is also part of "our way of proceeding.")

"Consolation," if this occurred in the person unto whom Jesuits ministered, was the surest sign that all was well. Nadal, Polanco, and others had learned from the *Exercises* what this meant and how central it was. They had, in fact, learned it so well that I am tempted to dub their ministry a "ministry of consolation" and their spirituality a "spirituality of consolation." Their way of proceeding in the help of souls was to listen intently to the movements of consolation and desolation in those they sought out to help and to instill in those persons the discretion and courage to follow what "the Creator and Lord in person communicates to the devout soul in quest of the divine will," as the fifteenth annotation of the *Exercises* has it [15].

So much more could be said about consolation, but let me turn the subject over to Nadal and to Peter Faber. Nadal is commenting on the ministries of the Society listed in the Formula of the Institute, i.e., in the bull *Exposcit debitum* of Julius III, 1550. He has already spoken about preaching, the *Exercises,* and the teaching of catechism. When he comes to the words "especially the spiritual consolation of Christ's faithful through the hearing of confessions," he says:

> These words—"especially spiritual consolation"—refer to *all* the primary ministries of the Society. They at the same time mean that we are not to be content in those ministries only with what is necessary for salvation but pursue beyond it the perfection and consolation of our neighbor. For spiritual consolation is the best index of a person's spiritual progress. The word *especially* means that there are other ends we must pursue, but this one in the first place, as our primary intention and goal. If we do not have time and resources for both this and the others, we should omit doing them, apply

2

Predicting the Past, Looking Back for the Future

John W. Padberg, S.J.

"There is nothing so difficult to predict as the past." Since history does not get at the past "just as it really happened," every historical study is in some part an interpretation. That is true of this presentation too. It is a bridge from the historical past to the contemporary with only several moments in our Jesuit history highlighted. In so doing, we shall, as Dr. Samuel Johnson said, "rise to the grandeur of generalizations." Another essay in this book deals with the distinctiveness of Jesuit spirituality in the sixteenth century, and it notes quite importantly that that distinctive spirituality was inserted into a tradition already more than fifteen hundred years old. The tradition of Christian spirituality helped shape Jesuit spirituality in the sixteenth century and on to our own day, often exerting a pressure on it to conform to older ways of looking at things. That pressure continued to exist very strongly until the truly revolutionary changes of Vatican II, and it continues to exert an influence, often salutary, sometimes problematic, even after those changes.

Note: The source of and/or stimulus to some of the material in this essay comes from the work of the late Michel de Certeau, S.J., especially his part of the article "Jésuites" in the *Dictionnaire de Spiritualité*.

"Spirituality" in this essay means the way an individual (*my* spirituality) or here a group (*the* spirituality of the Society of Jesus) conceives of and puts into practice a relationship to God as it calls on its understanding of the Gospel, the tradition of the Church, the charism of the founder of the group, the traditions of the group itself, and the activities, both historical and current, of the group. Spirituality, therefore, includes action and reflection, prayer and activity, change and constancy in the specific way that a group deals with its relationship with God. The history of a spirituality is not simply a history of the literature written about that spirituality. While that is good and instructive, there are also other ways of looking at a spirituality. One such way is to look at the structure or organization within which a particular spirituality became possible and was lived out. Another way, especially in this instance for the Society of Jesus, is to look at the activities of Jesuits themselves as fashioners of and witnesses to their spirituality.

This present essay will, in its first part, consider two examples of such structuring of Jesuit spirituality in its historical circumstances. The second and briefer part will consider some generalizations and some questions perhaps useful for our own day. The first example involves a crisis of growth, the second a crisis of refounding. Toward the end of each of these periods certain characteristics of Jesuit spirituality were fixed for a long time to come. As a matter of fact, those characteristics perdured right up to our own days. For ease of reference, those two periods will be designated by the names of the Fathers General of the time. The first, the period of the crisis of growth, includes Everard Mercurian and Claudio Acquaviva. They were generals respectively from 1574 to 1581 and from 1581 to 1615, a total of forty-two years. Then the next general, Muzio Vitelleschi, for twenty more years, from 1615 to 1635 carried forward those characteristics of the Mercurian-Acquaviva period. The second example, the period of the crisis of refounding, includes the generals Luigi Fortis and Jan Roothaan. Fortis was general from 1820 to 1829, and Roothaan from 1829 to 1853, a total of thirty-three years. And then Peter Beckx followed as general for the next thirty years, 1853 to 1883. So, just as the first example covers sixty-two years, the second includes a sixty-three year span.

To begin, we do not easily recognize how relatively un-structured was the spiritual preparation and development of the men who came into the Society of Jesus in its early years. It is indeed true that distinctive elements of Jesuit spirituality already existed, such as, preeminently, the Spiritual Exercises themselves, the understanding of a world that, however flawed, was by nature fundamentally good, the radically apostolic/pastoral nature of that spirituality, and the desire to treat each person individually at the here and now stage of that person's spiritual development. But the way in which these and other elements were presented to the neophyte Jesuits who were entering the order in large numbers and the way in which as a coherent whole those elements were lived out by the Jesuits who were quickly "sent on mission" was still amorphous, lacking a reflected-upon organization and unity. The primary and sometimes only structured initial formation seems to have come through the Spiritual Exercises. Even then there may have been some Jesuits who in the very, very early years of the Society did not even make the full Exercises. The first truly organized structure for the formation of new members came with the institution of novitiates apart from the ordinary houses of the Society. That took place under Francis Borgia who was general after Ignatius and James Laynez, from 1565 to 1572, in the first detailed instructions on how to be a novice master. Along with those instructions as organizing influence, there were especially the exhortations of Jerome Nadal, particularly those on the Constitutions. At the same time, however, other factors contributed to the atmosphere and ambience of early Jesuit life. For example, there were the seriousness of religious life following the Council of Trent, a certain type of romantic vigor and rigor about this new order, and the unusual features which distinguished it. All of those contributed to an atmos-phere, an atmosphere but not yet a real structure, in the very early years of Jesuit spirituality. At the same time, all the way up through the generalate of Borgia, there was an extraordi-nary amount of coming and going into and out of the Society.

One of the more extreme examples is that of a relative of one of the early generals who entered and left three different times. Much more importantly, although there was already much that was distinctive in practice about the spirituality of the Society, there was as yet little theological reflection on the proper nature of that distinctive Jesuit spirituality.

The period in which structuring began on a rather large scale is that of Mercurian who, as noted earlier, was general from 1573 to 1581. The first and extremely important circumstance in which that structuring took place was the phenomenal growth of the Society. The same circumstance was also present after the Restoration and in Jesuit life in the United States in the nineteenth century. Stop to recall that in 1556, at the death of Ignatius, there were only about one thousand Jesuits. Eighteen years later, in 1574, there were four times as many, almost four thousand Jesuits. How does one provide a proper training for those men? How does one see that the spirit of the Society and the Institute of the Society, that is, the written documents, the way of life, the activities, the attitudes, how does one see that all of those are inculcated in and assimilated by a fourfold increase in numbers? By 1579, the Society had grown another twenty percent to better than five thousand plus members. In that year there were twenty-one provinces with an average of two hundred and thirty-eight members per province. Those men lived and worked in ten professed houses, one hundred and forty-four colleges, thirty-three residences and twelve novitiates separate from those other institutions. Remember that all of this took place within forty years of the foundation of the Jesuits. Obviously, this phenomenal growth imposed its own pressures on the Society.

The second characteristic of this period of structuring under Mercurian and Acquaviva was the opening up of huge new apostolates to this extraordinary number of Jesuits. The very early Jesuits had mostly served in Italy, Spain, Portugal and somewhat, with difficulty, in France and in the Empire. It was during the later years of Borgia, and especially under Mercurian, that the Society moved in strength into northern Europe and really encountered the Protestant Reformation. It is also in that period of Mercurian's generalate that the Society moved in great numbers into the Far East and into Latin America and, in addition, took on a work for which it was initially reluctant and which was taken on only at the insistence of the pope, that is, the responsibility for twenty major pontifical seminaries in Europe. With all of that apostolic activity confided to the Jesuits, precisely because they were Jesuits, the question arose among them, "What is it to be a Jesuit?" "What is distinctive about our Institute, our way of life, our spirituality?"

Third, in the attempt to set up structures under Mercurian, problems existed which will sound very familiar for our own day. The first of them was the problem of working with the powerful, the extremely powerful in some instances, such as when a Jesuit worked as a confessor in one of the royal courts. How did that square with the primitive simplicity of Ignatius and the first companions? Another question consistently raised dealt with the amount of money spent on the apostolates, especially upon "buildings, buildings, buildings" as one of the fathers general complained, especially upon the magnificent baroque churches in which the apostolate of preaching, for which the Society was justly renowned, increasingly was carried on. How did that square with the spirit of poverty urged by Ignatius? Yet, remember that Ignatius himself had asked Michelangelo to build the Gesu, the principal Jesuit church, at the seat of the Society in Rome. A third problem arose from the necessities of the apostolate, the ways in which, especially in mission lands and in the lands of "the heretics," one had to have a certain freedom of action, such as in the work of Campion in England or of Possevino in Sweden and Russia. How did that square with the increasing number of very large houses with large numbers of Jesuits in them, the necessity of coordinating the community life and the apostolic work of those people, often enough in the schools, and the almost inevitable imposition of a daily order signaled by multiple rules and bells? Perhaps most importantly, there was the problem of the tension between a certain number of Jesuits who were convinced that the religious life could not be lived without serious penance, poverty, and recollection and who sought more of those characteristics in Jesuit houses and those other Jesuits who maintained that Ignatius wanted a common life in which people were not distinguished by singularity of penance or poverty or recollection but by a common life that was responsive principally to the external needs of the apostolate.

Among the ways in which Mercurian attempted to structure an as yet inchoate spirituality was an insistence on solid formation in the novitiate, regular order in the apostolic houses, the practice of specific virtues, the examination of conscience, the renovation of vows, and the practice of particular devotions. Does not this sound familiar to those Jesuits who remember from past years the regular reading at meals in the community dining room?

It was not, however, a case of Mercurian alone insisting on these. Most of the newly beginning Jesuit spiritual writings of his time mirrored this understanding that in some way the Society, growing by leaps and bounds, had to be sure of maintaining both the spirit of its founder and the nature of religious life. On this latter matter, some superiors in Spain had been all too rigorous; they wanted to use flogging and even jail in order to maintain the discipline of religious life. Fortunately, they got nowhere with this. There was a great fear of the deformation of the particular spirit of the Society and of its apostolic spirituality, still a rather new phenomenon, but also a fear of minimizing age-old practices of religious life. Mercurian responded with a two-fold approach. On the one hand, for example, he discouraged and in some instances forbade, the reading of spiritual writers other than those who were Jesuits and certainly the reading, without the permission of the superior, of the Rhineland mystics of the thirteenth and fourteenth centuries, people such as Suso or Tauler or Gertrude. They were regarded as foreign to the apostolic character and spirit of Jesuit life. There were quite specific restrictions placed by the general on the ways of prayer taught by Jesuits such as Baltasar Alvarez and Cordeses. The way of prayer that they were teaching seem to be regarded, as a matter of fact quite unfairly, as too contemplative, not ascetic enough, leaving the passions and the affections as disordered afterwards as they had been before. On the other hand, from this period of Mercurian, too, date the first formal edition of the Rules of the Society of Jesus (in 1580), a revision of an earlier set of rules of Borgia, the regular conferences on the obligations of religious life as such, with a greater emphasis on the vows and particular virtues rather than on the vocation and life of the Society as arising out of particular Jesuit apostolates.

If Mercurian was the first to have to confront in a consistent manner this question of structure, Acquaviva was the general who had to deal with it even more acutely and for a much longer and much more tumultuous period. He served from 1581 to 1615, the longest generalate in the history of the Society. Acquaviva is arguably the most important superior general other than Ignatius, and yet no full-scale biography has been written of him in any language. In that generalate of thirty-five years, the Society grew from five thousand members in 1580 to thirteen thousand members in 1615. Again remember that the latter year is still less than seventy-five years since the death of Ignatius. With that growth in numbers came also increased specializations as Jesuits went into all kinds of new apostolates and ministries, and an increased regionalization or localization with the growth in numbers and size of provinces, along with a growth in national consciousness and some of the effects that went with it. The diversity and specialization of exterior works and the need for a continuity of a single interior spirit presented a continuing problem of expressing and living out their relationships. To this, the major reaction was the growth and codification of rules pertaining to the internal life of the Society. Some examples, in chronological order will make this clear. After the 1580 rules for the master of novices, regulating the life of the novitiates, there came in 1581 the obligation of an hour of daily prayer for everyone in the Society. From 1585 to 1599 the *Ratio Studiorum* took shape. In 1593-94 the tertianship was structured and regularized. Note that it took fifty years from the death of Ignatius before the general provision of the Constitutions for a *"schola affectus"* was actually put in to a structure, the structure that perdured in its essentials all the way up to the 31st General Congregation in 1965-66. In 1608, the semi-annual triduum was imposed as an antecedent to the regular renovation of vows. In 1608, too, came the regularization and the spread everywhere of the juniorate and its isolation, along with the novitiate, from other houses of the Society. Again in 1608, an *annus mirablis*, the annual eight-day retreat was imposed upon everyone. In 1611, came a document revealingly entitled "For the Solidarity and Uniformity of Doctrine throughout the Entire Society." The secretary of the Society at the time remarked that "we are engaged in spiritual administration."

But this left the major question still unanswered; How does one use the apostolic works and the characteristics of those works as the common language expressing the spirit of the Society? This could become increasingly difficult because the Society no longer engaged simply in the type of generalized, overall apostolates enunciated in the Formula of the Institute, such as preaching the word of God, giving the Spiritual Exercises, teaching Christianity to the unlettered, and spiritual conversations. And it no longer had simply those generalized apostolates of the early years and their characteristics as the experience out of which the vocabulary for expressing the spirit of the Society arose. Increasingly, on the contrary, Jesuit apostolic works were becoming tied to local conditions, social circumstances, national characteristics, and increasing professionalization. Jesuits in particular ministries were talking in the language of those ministries in ways that Jesuits in other ministries simply either did not understand or did not have the opportunity to understand. All of this gave rise increasingly to the urgent question: What is proper to the Society? What is distinctive about it, and, especially, what in its activities makes for a distinctive spirituality? To put the problem in a single and perhaps complicated sentence: How does one define or describe a Jesuit spirituality of a "mixed" life that is both active and contemplative and at the same time how define or describe an "interior life" particular to the Society which is distinct from its "works" but which finds its raison d'être and its vocabulary in those apostolic works? That is the problem which plagued this period of the Society's history and perhaps also presses upon its life today. A solution was attempted in trying to construct a life interior to and specific to the

Society by making increasingly sharp distinctions between those things which were *nostrum* and those which were *alienum*, the latter sometimes very interestingly called *peregrinum*. *Nostrum* is that which was ours; *alienum* was that which belonged to others; *peregrinum* had the meaning of that which was temporary or passing in the life of the Society. Such a use of this last term, *peregrinum*, is ironic in the context of Nadal's use of the same term when speaking of Jesuits essentially as travelers or pilgrims and of the whole world as the house or residence proper to Jesuits.

Increasingly the question was asked, "What is ours' and what is "foreign to the spirit of the Institute?" The overall objective here was to put together, if possible, a common universe of discourse, arising out of common ways of doing and viewing things. How did the Society attempt to do that? Some examples may make clear the process. First, this is the period, from the late 1580's on to the end of the century and then on into the next century, when with the publication of the various Directories of the Spiritual Exercises the Society tried to set down a common method of doing that spiritual work most distinctive of the Society. The Directories increasingly codified that work. Secondly, an increasingly official portrait of the "Founder" of the Society and of his spirit came into being. In 1572 Pedro Ribadeneyra had published his life of Ignatius. Acquaviva during his generalate asked Ribadeneyra to revise it, which he supposedly somewhat reluctantly did, and which he made more serviceable to the needs of Acquaviva's time by different emphases. Then, too, Acquaviva arranged for the publication in 1585 of one of the more famous lives of Ignatius, that of Maffei. It is much more objective, more official, less familial, less personal, more traditional in spirit and language than Ribadeneyra's. It had been started in 1573, the year after the earlier biography came out, in a sense as counterpoint to Ribadeneyra's, which with some informality had more of the spirit of the "Fioretti" of St. Francis than was judged appropriate for a biography of "the Founder." Even before that, back in the 1570s Gonçalves de Camara had added in the Portuguese version of his originally Spanish portrait of Ignatius recollections about the firmness and discipline of government by Ignatius. As another example, it is instructive to look at the changes in iconography over the decades, in the ways Ignatius is portrayed in paintings. It includes portraits of a man dressed as a knight or pilgrim, a superior of the Society in Roman clerical garb, a priest in Mass vestments, a lawgiver pointing to a book, the *Constitutions*, which he is holding in his hand, with both man and book illuminated by rays from above as though both are guaranteed of divine inspiration. A persistent example of such iconography of supernatural intervention is that of Ignatius writing the *Spiritual Exercises* at Manresa in the presence of the Blessed Virgin who is dictating them to him. A further step in developing the portrait of the founder came in the way in which one conceived of fidelity to the spirit of the founder. Was the fidelity to that spirit achieved by following the example of the life of the founder or by following the texts and rules that the founder wrote? The answer was not and is not an easy "either/or," but the second of those two possibilities was increasingly emphasized. Later in the seventeenth century, some of the French "spirituals" in the Society had a vigorous reaction to that choice. One of them remarked that fidelity is not conformity to institutions and knowledge, but rather it is an interior light and spiritual knowledge "of the greatness of this great saint, hidden even from most of his children." But a word of caution is necessary there too. Notice how individualistic and idiosyncratic this can turn out to be if each member of the Society is simply following his own inner light.

The third means of attempting to put together a common universe of discourse was the multiplication of a spiritual literature proper to Jesuits specifically, *ad usum nostrorum,* "for the use of ours." Through the seventeenth century there was a plethora of such publications, rules, maxims, sayings, apothegms, formulae, epitomes.

Fourth, and food for thought, there was a gradual increase in the place of the then current general in the published collections of the writings of the early Jesuits. Perhaps most instructive in this regard in a 1609 edition of the letters of the fathers general to the Society. That collection contains twelve letters, two by Ignatius, one by Laynez, one by Borgia, and eight by Acquaviva. More instructive yet, of the six hundred and twenty pages in that collection five hundred are taken up by the letters of Acquaviva. Lest one feel superior today, it is interesting to note that the Society was willing in the 1930s to put resources and money into a one-volume edition of the selected writings of Father General Ledechowski translated into English fifty years before it got around to putting into English the complete works of Ignatius in one volume.

It is too facile, however, to denigrate or to minimize the above actions and think what they were attempting was foolish or unimportant. That increasing emphasis on an internal life specific to the Society helped to make possible at the same time the extraordinary variety of Jesuit external apostolates, the schools, the missions, the retreats, the work in the natural sciences, the originality of cultural adaptations, the court confessors, the explorers, the "reductions" of Latin America, the daring of the Chinese and Malabar rites, the professionalization that made possible such an extraordinary variety of external ministries with their own rules which did not depend on religious life as such. The firmly developed skeletal and closely articulated interior structure of the Jesuit edifice allowed it to be adapted in its external activities to almost any purpose.

There was, however, a price to be paid, and there were plenty of disagreements on the extent to which the cost of the demands of these external apostolates diminished the treasure of the original charism of the Society. There were disagreements on prayer, to begin with. It is very instructive to read Acquaviva's letter on prayer of 1590 or his letter on the liturgy in 1612 and to learn how they bear echoes of the controversies inside the general's curia itself, among the general's assistants, for example Hoffaeus versus Maggio, about what was and what was not proper to Ignatian prayer. Under the rubric of action versus contemplation they debated the issues involved. There had been popular booklets for the laity, for Jesuits themselves, for other religious, earlier in the history of the Society, but the great doctrinal texts about the life and spirituality of the Society came only after about 1605-1615. Earlier in the Society there had been much emphasis on Jesuits reading the fathers of the Church. Then some began to ask whether they were relevant to such an apostolic order in the seventeenth century and whether there was something that should be proper to the Society as such. It was after this period that some of the great classic texts within Jesuit spirituality came onto the scene, for example, Alvarez de Paz's *De vita spirituali*, Suarez's *De virtute et statu religionis*, Coton's *Interieur occupation*, de la Puente's *Life of Baltasar Alvarez*, and, most notably, Rodriguez's *The Practice of Perfection and Christian Virtues*, dealing with the spiritual life proper to this particular apostolic order. A brief aside: Sometime one ought to reread Rodriguez in the socio-religious context of his time. It is one of the great classics of the "modern" spirituality of the seventeenth century, and it had enduring influence up to the middle of the twentieth century. It is unfortunate that twentieth-century Jesuit reading of it took place usually only in the novitiate, and as a result it has not received its due in several ways.

Besides the crisis in prayer, several crises in government and structure also erupted in the Society. Far too complicated to detail here, they arose especially out of the conviction, especially on the part of some disaffected Spanish Jesuits, that they knew best what the Society ought to be and to do. Pope Sixtus V and the Spanish court concurred in the plan to change the Society's governmental structures, but ultimately Acquaviva prevailed and satisfied the pope. Then later the troubles again found concrete expression in the fifth general congregation in 1593-94 which in effect was forced on the Society by Clement VIII. Again, no fundamental changes were made, but in all these years there were writings aplenty on prayer, on spirituality, on government. To take only two examples, there were books with titles such as *Advice on What To Do to Reform the Society of Jesus* or *The Great Faults in the Government of the Society of Jesus*.

The generalates of Mercurian and Acquaviva profoundly affected the Society for all of its centuries to follow. None of the questions that were raised here, among the many others that might also have been mentioned, were fully answered then or later. In addition, the next general, Muzio Vitelleschi, for the next twenty years after Acquaviva further built on the foundation and within the boundaries that had been firmly established by his predecessors. The Society was governed and its strictness solidified by these three generals, Mercurian, Acquaviva, and Vitelleschi.

So, too, with the fathers general of the second period to be dealt with here. Luigi Fortis and Jan Roothaan governed the Society for thirty-three years from 1820 to 1829 and from 1829 to 1853, and then Peter Beckx for another thirty years from 1853 to 1883, for a total of sixty-three consecutive years. This section of the essay will deal with some of the external circumstances of the restored Society and then with its spirituality. With the restored Society of Jesus, just as earlier with the expanding Society of Jesus, those circumstances of personnel, of apostolic works, and of characteristics of the time, were quite special to begin with.

The questions of personnel included first of all, numbers or growth. At the restoration of the Society in 1814 there were, at most, about six hundred Jesuits in the world. At the death of Roothaan in 1853, there were five thousand Jesuits. Thirty years after that, in 1883 at the death of Beckx, there were eleven thousand Jesuits. At the end of the seventy years from the restoration to the death of Beckx there were twenty times as many Jesuits as there had been at the restoration. With that growth in personnel came all kinds of questions and problems. How does one deal with the preparation of Jesuits in the circumstances of such utterly explosive growth? How was one to deal with the variety of personnel in the Society at its restoration? There were, first, the veterans, men who had been in the Society before the suppression, who had persisted in hope and who, now quite advanced in years, were again part of the universal Society. A second group consisted of recruits who entered the interim Society early in the nineteenth century from the utterly changed environment of a revolutionary and post-revolutionary Europe. Many of them, as was Roothaan, had been trained in Russia in that interim Society. They had paid great personal prices for an extraordinary fidelity to the idea of the Society. They had a hyper-acute sense of what fidelity to the old Society meant, although they had never experienced it, because it was only with that sense that they had been able to maintain themselves in Russia. Thirdly, there were mature men who had not been in the Society before but who had belonged to the Society of the Sacred Heart or the Fathers of the Faith, two organizations founded with the specific purpose that, if the Society of Jesus were ever restored, their members would come into it. Some of them had unusual ideas, to say the least, of what was appropriate or special to the Society. Lastly, there was the fourth group of completely new recruits who, from the restoration on for the next half century, entered in large numbers.

Everywhere the renascent Society was so overwhelmed by the works that were offered to it that for many new entrants there was at best a makeshift novitiate or almost no novitiate at all. Everywhere Jesuits were asked to take up old apostolates again or to take on new ones. As an example, the province of France alone was asked to take on in the first ten years after the restoration eighty-three colleges. With a membership of three hundred and fifty men, it did accept "only" eleven such schools. Other provinces had similar experiences across the whole range of apostolates.

All of this began in 1814 with the general Thaddeus Brzozowski, forbidden by the Russian government to leave that country and therefore with a vicar governing in Rome, with questions about the work and the characteristics of the Society unanswered, and with some members of the papal curia wanting to change certain characteristics of the Society to make it less an independent religious order than it had been.

In those circumstances, Luigi Fortis in 1820 became the first elected general after the restoration. He was elected partly because he had been a member of the Society before the suppression and the symbol and reality of continuity were immensely important. But that 20th General Congregation itself began with a serious controversy between two groups of delegates with differing ideas on the Society and the Constitutions and on the validity of the vows of the pre-Restoration members from Russia. The controversy was resolved, but only with sharp debate in the congregation, the expulsion of several men from the Society, and the deprivation of office of the vicar general himself. Only then was the new general elected. The congregation immediately recognized the overriding need to structure again Jesuit life and activity. Understandably, it legislated for the restoration and practice in full force and vigor of the Constitutions and the Spiritual Exercises. But the congregation also decided that absolutely all the decrees, rules, and ordinances of all the previous general congregations and of all the previous generals were also to come back into force. This, too, was understandable, given the concern that this be not a new Society of Jesus but the same one as had existed before. One might, however, question such a wholesale and unnuanced reestablishment in a world that in forty years had, with the French Revolution, changed so overwhelmingly. The congregation went on to pass decrees on poverty, on the reprinting and study of the Institute, on the training of novices, and on down to details such as how and when public penances were to be performed in the dining room. Structure was absolutely necessary, so the delegates thought, and in many ways it was, but so detailed a structure could and in some cases did lead to immobilism. Fortis worked mightily to nurture the growth of this very frail shoot, and, given the obstacles, including on the exterior a fanatical anti-Jesuitism exacerbated by all the old legends about Jesuitry, he did very well in these very early years of the renascent Society.

In 1829 the man who was to be the real refounder of the restored Society of Jesus was elected general, Jan Roothaan. When elected, he was, after Acquaviva, the youngest general the Society has had. Like Acquaviva, he had to face a crisis of structure and of growth. Despite the decrees of the previous congregation, organization was embryonic, structure was makeshift, and training was often haphazard for at least twenty to twenty-five years after the restoration, while at the same time new recruits came in a steady stream. It could be regarded as a miracle of God's grace that the Society of Jesus actually got started again and grew so rapidly.

Roothaan spent a great portion of his generalate calling the Society back to its authentic traditions of apostolate and spirituality, with the latter meaning, as earlier described in this essay, the way in which a group conceives of and puts into practice a relationship to God as it calls on its understanding of the Gospel, the traditions of the Church, the charism of the founder of the group, the traditions of the group itself, and the activities, both historical and current of the group. All of these had to be rebuilt. The four central traditions at which he worked were the Spiritual Exercises, the theory and practice of the educational apostolate, the missionary spirit and endeavor of the Society, and the inculcation of Jesuit spirituality and the consolidation of the religious life in the houses of the Society. His successor, Peter Beckx, carried on essentially the same program.

In 1834 Roothaan published one of the more important letters ever written on the study and giving of the Spiritual Exercises, and he followed that up a year later with a new Latin translation, far more faithful to the Spanish of the original text by Ignatius than the ornate and long-used Latin Vulgate version by de Freux. Some time later Roothaan's own notes were published as a book, *De Ratione Meditandi.* In some ways his work inculcated a rigid and literalist use of the Exercises, but it was an understandable reaction to the fanciful interpretations which had proliferated over the centuries and to the hiatus in study and practice during the suppression. For the educational apostolate, the general congregation of 1820 had mandated a revision of the *Ratio Studiorum.* Fortis could not finish the work, and so Roothaan took it up; the result was the *Ratio* of 1832. Although it did somewhat recognize the post-Revolutionary changes in the world and although it was never officially promulgated by a general congregation, this revision put a structure back into the apostolate of education. It was certainly too rigid a structure for the schools of North America, and in reality it could not truly be implemented here no matter what lip service was paid to it.

The external missionary endeavor, which had so rapidly expanded under Mercurian and Acquaviva, received the same impetus under Fortis and most especially under Roothaan. In 1821 the first new recruits came to the United States from Europe to what eventually became the Missouri Province. The roster of new Jesuit missionary fields is impressive: 1831 Syria, 1834 India, 1836 Argentina and other parts of Latin America,

1844 Madagascar, 1848 Australia, 1852 French Guyana. An immense spirit of zeal moved Jesuits out into the nineteenth century world. They took advantage of the second great colonial expansion, just as they had of the first one in the sixteenth and seventeenth centuries. That earlier expansion took Jesuits under the aegis of Spain and Portugal to all their possessions. So now in the nineteenth century that endeavor took place especially under the aegis of France and England as they established or extended their colonies. Then, of course, opening up to immigrants from all over Europe was that great new mission land of the United States. One never knew how different it might be in this country from the old assurances of Europe, and, while the writ of the Jesuit rule was meant to be valid here as elsewhere, the improvisations in the apostolate were often disconcerting to and misunderstood by Rome. The differences brought all kinds of reactions, from the lament of an early Jesuit "visitor" to Fordham that American students were constitutionally incapable of learning Greek to the exemption from the Constitutions given to St. Louis University to charge tuition for its classes because, among other reasons, it was explained, such is the character of the Americans that they hold of little value that which they get for nothing. On that exemption, "until the times improve," all the Jesuit schools of the whole world lived until in 1965 the 31st General Congregation changed the Society's legislation.

All of this internal restructuring and the frenetic pace at which external apostolates were offered and taken on raised at times for Roothaan and then for Beckx the same kinds of problems as those of Mercurian's and Acquaviva's times. The needs of the apostolate and the needs of religious life were regularly in tension. For both Roothaan and Beckx, there was the additional problem of the constant political upheavals which during their years in office directly affected the Society. The Jesuits were expelled from twenty different places in the course of Roothaan's and Beckx's generalates, and Roothaan himself had to go into exile from Rome at the time of the 1848 Revolution. The reaction, of course, was that the interior life had to be deepened, and the internal discipline of the Society had to be made even more rigorous when the Jesuits could again regroup. Studies and tertianship and fidelity to the founder's spirit and the observance of the rules, even if Jesuits had to live dispersed in small communities, were emphasized over and over and over again. Those expulsions and other persecutions also tended to produce an understandable but overly defensive reaction in the Society itself and a further resistance to change.

The sources which fed Jesuit spirituality in the restored Society of Jesus in its first fifty or sixty years were both general to the Catholic world and specific to the Jesuits. Among those general sources were Sacred Scripture (read and understood very literally) and in the early years a good amount of reading of the Fathers of the church. Overall in the world of that time there was a great taste for the Middle Ages and a heavily romanticized version of what those "Christian centuries" had been like. Witnesses to that sensibility were the many neo-Romanesque and neo-Gothic churches built at that time, the apostolates which were regularly designated by the term "crusades," such as "Eucharistic Crusades," the studies of the Middle Ages that a good number of European Jesuits undertook. But just as in the earlier period, the Society asked what was properly a Jesuit family spirituality. In response, there was much re-editing and republishing of classic works from the old Society, including letters of the generals. The return to the Spiritual Exercises was, as earlier mentioned, much more literal than before. From the first days of the novitiate, the Summary of the Constitutions (seldom the Constitutions themselves) and the plethora of particular rules were studied and the ordinary ways of prayer and of the spiritual life were emphasized as far more important than any that might be extraordinary. The formal study of the Exercises was something new and more characteristic of the restored Society than of the pre-Suppression Jesuits. That study took the form of books, commentaries, pamphlets, directories, volumes of meditation, and the beginning of work on critical text editions.

Several important external activities or apostolates helped structure that spirituality. First of all, there was spiritual writing. There were few really substantial writings of this type, that is serious theological works in spirituality, from 1814 until after 1860 or 1870. Rather, there were many practical prayer books, novenas, manuals of devotions, many works that responded to "the trials of the Church and the trials of the Society." For example, the devotion to the Sacred Heart of Jesus that had existed before the nineteenth century at times took on in prayerbooks and novenas the particular cast of devotion to the agonizing heart of Jesus. A great number of Jesuit biographies and autobiographies and intimate spiritual journals were published. Such published works had not been common in the old Society, but one can list them by the dozens in the new Society. (Interestingly enough, however, neither the *Spiritual Journal* of Favre nor even the *Spiritual Diary* of Ignatius were translated until late in the century). Such intimate personal publications grew in part out of the sensibility of romanticism with its interest in the individual and in the interior state of such an individual.

The giving of the Spiritual Exercises was itself a great, external, spiritual apostolate. Periodic retreats had been obligatory for Jesuits from 1608 on. In the 1700s this practice came into vogue for other religious, and it became a generalized practice for them and for priests in the nineteenth century. With the restoration, Jesuits began to give preached and group retreats not only to religious but also to lay people. In the old Society they had not been that common except in a very few places. The first closed preached retreat for laity in the new Society was probably a group retreat in Rome in 1825. Such preached retreats became generalized in the 1870s and 1880s, with special houses for them after 1900.

Another important apostolate, an attempt to respond to the question of how to bring to lay people a spirituality of apostolic activity, was the Marian congregation or sodality. In the old Society those congregations had been one of the more successful, specific forms of something more generally widespread, the artisanal, commercial and religious confraternities or guilds for adult laymen and priests. All such guilds or confraternities, not just the religious type, were destroyed by the Revolution. When Pope Leo XII gave the old Roman College back to the Society after the restoration, he also entrusted to it the reestablishment of the Marian congregations which had first been established at that school. There followed in the nineteenth century a craze for affiliation with that first sodality with all of the indulgences attached to it. Then Jesuits established sodalities principally in their schools, and the congregations became an organization for adolescents rather than for the adults for which they had originally been intended. Finally, an area of great influence for the restored Society was religious orders and congregations. In the old Society, Jesuit involvement with them as such was small. After the restoration, many newly-founded, active apostolic orders of men and women derived much of their structure from the example of the Society as such as an order. Indeed, Jesuits were directly involved in founding or assisting in the establishment of a great number of those congregations, especially of women.

How in the sensibility of the nineteenth century Society did all of this external activity and the internal spiritual life of the Society come together? The central symbol of the attempt to put them together was devotion to the Sacred Heart as embodied in the Apostleship of Prayer and the League of the Sacred Heart. The Frenchman, François Gautrelet, founded the Apostleship in 1844 precisely to give Jesuit scholastics a sense of the apostolic worth of their lives of study and prayer. Henri Ramière in 1861 enlarged its vision and extended its scope, maintaining that all Christians ought to involve themselves in restoring the social reign of Christ. While he saw this as indeed a religious task, quite frankly for him that also involved, at least in France, a restoration of the monarchy. But the devotion quickly far surpassed any such ideological orientation and spread so widely and deeply that from the middle of the nineteenth century to a quarter century ago, at times with some aberrations but most often quite simply and affectingly, it became the principal hallmark of devotional Catholicism. How this particular devotion to Christ on the part of the Society and the Church became so overwhelmingly widespread in the nineteenth century still has to be told in detail. But however it happened, the devotion was testimony to the absolutely central point about Jesuit spirituality and Jesuit apostolates, and that is Jesus himself.

From Ignatius to today, how in practice one puts Jesus

at the center of Jesuit life and work has varied with the times, but that central place itself has been constant. There have been other constants, too, in the history of Jesuit spirituality, as the particular moments of the interrelationship of spirituality and structure dealt with in this essay give evidence.

Because those constants merit special attention in our own circumstances today, a brief treatment of them makes up the last part of this essay. First, regularly there has been a need, or at least a strong desire, for some kind of known, recognized, central structure or armature or framework for Jesuit spirituality, however we conceive of the particulars of that spirituality. This is especially true at stressful moments, for example, with Mercurian and Acquaviva at the crisis of growth, and with Fortis and Roothaan at the crisis of restoration. In the stresses of a post-Vatican II church, when all of its members, Jesuits and others, are still attempting to understand and live out the implications of the council, that need, that desire, will continue to be with us. Secondly, if there is some such central framework and, just as importantly, a language with which to talk about it, then there can be variety, change, difference, adaptation, in the flesh that we put on the skeleton, in the rooms we put in the interior of the building, in the cladding we put on the exterior of that framework, in the ways in which individually and communally we live out that spirituality, and in the ways in which we undertake apostolic works in accord with it. But, thirdly, and this complicates the situation, that structure or framework itself also changes. The armature is not so much like the steel framework of a building as it is like the human skeletal structure, which itself also changes and grows.

Next, how does the Society of Jesus, collectively as the Society and individually in its member Jesuits, express the essential elements of that structure? That will always be a continuing question and an ongoing task to be worked at because it involves quite important considerations. Do Jesuit apostolic works determine or at least specify the spirituality of the Society, or does the spirituality determine or at least specify the apostolic works? For example, a "visitor" to one of the American provinces in the nineteenth century reputedly urged that more men and more resources be put into the apostolate of education than into the apostolate to native Americans. Obviously, there are reasons for which one might choose either of these works. But the reason he gave for his choice was that it was easier in the colleges to maintain the common religious life and spirituality of the Society, with the rules and customs and prayers at specified times, than it was in the mission setting. In this instance, the spirituality as he understood it determined the work.

As in Acquaviva's time, there is a continuing problem of how the Society uses the original, foundational, generalized apostolic works noted in the Formula of the Institute as the common structure of its spirituality when those works become increasingly specialized by time, place, professional requirements, and social conditions. What is "ours?" What is "our way of proceeding?" What is "foreign to our Institute?" Is anything foreign to it? How is that question decided? Fifth, it is not so much disagreement here but reluctance seriously to investigate past roots and to assess present situations and to imagine what the future might be and to talk with each other about those subjects that will push the Society of Jesus to structure a monolithic or unitary version of that spirituality and, therefore, in all likelihood an impoverished version.

Last, without recognition of the internal and external factors which affect the structuring of the spirituality of the Society of Jesus, Jesuits talk at cross purposes. Such factors include but are not limited to demographics, cultural and intellectual movements, politics, ecclesiastical attitudes and needs, and the climate or general attitude of the Society itself. Take demographics, to begin with. For example, the Society in the United States carries on formation programs now differently than in the past and with a different rationale. But the smaller number of Jesuits are among the factors that make such a change possible. When there were sixty men in a novitiate and two hundred in a theologate, the Society could not have done what it is now doing in formation. What would a province do in its formation program if it again had large numbers of men in each stage of it? To turn to cultural and intellectual climates, the baroque sensibility of the seventeenth century and the romantic sensibility of the nineteenth surely influenced the men who became Jesuits and influenced the Society itself. Do we take serious and explicit account of how the twentieth century American cultural and intellectual climates with their utilitarian individualist, democratizing currents impinge upon Jesuit spirituality today? In politics, the ascendancy of Spain was evident in the world and in the Church from the time of Ignatius through the time of Acquaviva. Later in the seventeenth and on into the eighteenth centuries France became ascendant, and one need only look at the growth and influence of French schools of spirituality, both generally and within the Society. But at the same time France continued the absolutist, centralizing political tradition of Spain, and that tradition exerted its influence on the Church and on the Society of Jesus. Should we not become more aware of what political currents in the modern world impinge upon the Society, upon its spirituality and its works today? In the Church of the late sixteenth century on, there was a continuing optimism at the success of the post-Tridentine reformation. In the nineteenth century there was an intransigent conservatism in the aftermath of what happened to the Church in the French Revolution. For the decade after Vatican II there was an extraordinary and perhaps naive optimism in the Church; there has been a sense of regrouping and retrenchment in the last fifteen years. How have those recent attitudes of the last twenty-five years affected the structures of Jesuit life and spirituality and apostolate? As for the Society itself, what has been its own internal climate or general attitude over the last quarter century, over the last ten years?

To conclude, from Ignatius on and for both of the periods treated in this essay and for Jesuits today the central questions are: How does the Society conceive and live out and transmit a spirituality which attempts to combine in its structuring a strong central authority with a widespread dispersion of members; an assured and stable interiority with a mobile, varying, fluid exteriority; a solidity of body and a continuity in "our way of proceeding" with a flexible adaptation for "the good of souls?" How does the Society multiply possibilities in its life and work while reasonably attempting to contain risk? How does one encourage the flexibility of the Society and of its members in order to serve the changing needs of the church and of the world and of its members themselves while at the same time maintaining for the individual Jesuit and for the group some kind of an anchorage or haven which does not excessively depend on the outside? This essay cannot in its brief compass presume to give answers to those questions. It can, however, attempt to keep them in the forefront of consciousness and perhaps make Jesuits individually and as a group begin to answer them.

Most importantly, this essay can recall that the central reference point of Jesuit spirituality is fixed on the following of Christ in his life, in his "helping of others" in the continuing community of life which is his church, and in the companionship in the Lord that is the Society of Jesus. The response particular to the Society is Jesuit spirituality itself, the specific ways in which out of its experience in all its differing places and times the Society of Jesus conceives and puts those relationships into practice in its life and works. The continuing challenge is how Jesuits are to imagine and structure for their Society such a spirituality faithful to its past, in real contact with its present, and looking to its future. If nothing is so difficult to predict as the past, nothing may be so necessary in the present as looking back for the future.

John W. Padberg, S.J.
Institute of Jesuit Sources
St. Louis, Missouri

3

Jesuit Spirituality: a Resource for Ministry Now and in the Future

Vincent T. O'Keefe, S.J.

That title can sound profoundly (and comfortably) vague and just about all-encompassing. It reminds me of a course I had as a novice which was entitled: Church History—Adam to Pius XII.

I promise to focus the topic as I talk about how our ministry flows out of our Ignatian spirituality, and how it influences what we're doing today in our ministry and what we will be doing in the future.

We are all familiar with the sources of Ignatian spirituality: the Spiritual Exercises, the Constitutions, the *Autobiography*, and the letters of St. Ignatius. Ignatian spirituality for me will always be involved with Father Pedro Arrupe, with his talks and writings during his generalate from 1965 to 1983, and with the life he led and leads today. To me he is Ignatian spirituality incarnate, in word and deed, in good times and in bad, in sickness and in health. The last three general congregations determined and spelled out for us the mission and apostolic goals of the Society today in continuity with our original Ignatian charism. These three general congregations form an integral whole and must be studied together. Pedro Arrupe played an essential and lively role in each of these congregations. In the 31st and 32nd General Congregations, he was physically present and active; at the 33rd, he was present in spirit and in his writings. Read the 33rd General Congregation and see how often it refers to Pedro Arrupe both in the main text and the footnotes.

When the 31st General Congregation elected Father Arrupe as superior general on May 22, 1965, the Second Vatican Council was still in session. It set down a double objective for religious institutes: a return to the sources of their particular charism (our Ignatian charism), and at the same time, an adaptation to the changed conditions of the times (cf. *Perfectae Caritatis*, n.2). These two principles were to guide the adaptation of our way of living and acting. They were at the center of attention of Pedro Arrupe, and of our last three general congregations, all during his eighteen years as superior general. In fact, one of the chief reasons for the appeal he exercised is that he combined these two principles to a remarkable degree in his own person. He showed unswerving loyalty to all that is fundamental in our lives, while at the same time he showed a knowledge of and interest in both the worldwide church that came alive at Vatican II and our modern world. He launched a great renewal in Ignatian sources and spirituality; but he also introduced a telex and Pepsi-Cola into the Jesuit Curia.

The 33rd General Congregation in 1983 publicly recognized Father Arrupe's role in these words: "The decrees of GC 31 (8, 13–17, 19) and GC 32 (2, 4, 11) as well as the writings of Father Arrupe have developed a spiritual doctrine at once profoundly rooted in the Gospel and our tradition and yet one which responds to the challenges of our times" (Documents of the 33rd General Congregation of the Society of Jesus published by The Institute of Jesuit Sources, St. Louis, 1984, p. 46, n.10).

Pedro Arrupe is of particular help in focusing our topic because of one of his favorite expressions, "Our Way of Proceeding." This phrase synthesized for Ignatius and his first companions the practical application of the Society's charism. Father Arrupe saw in this expression the means to attain the double objective that Vatican II had established for religious institutes, but to do this in a line of historical continuity. So I shall speak of our way of proceeding to indicate our Ignatian spirituality in its application to our ministries in our world today.

Our way of proceeding is based on a principle we can never forget and which Father Arrupe never tired of insisting on: the integration of the religious and apostolic aspects of our lives. The 31st General Congregation stated this most clearly in 1965: "Since the goal to which the Society directly tends is 'to help our own souls and the souls of our neighbor to attain the ultimate end for which they were created' (*Constitutions* 307), it is necessary that our life—of priests as well as scholastics and brothers—be individually apostolic and religious. This intimate connection between the religious and apostolic aspects in the Society ought to animate our whole way of living, praying, and working, and impress on it an apostolic character" (GC 31, decree 13, n.204).

This means that everything in our Society—our prayer, our vows, our intellectual and religious formation, our work, the internal organization of the Society—is ordered toward reaching its apostolic goal. This is clearly of capital importance for our way of proceeding lest by forgetting it, we lose our apostolic drive or nerve. It is also important because it is a characteristic of Ignatian spirituality not always understood outside our Society.

In a collection of writings which he characterized as his spiritual legacy, Pedro Arrupe's first contribution was a letter to the whole Society in 1976 entitled: "Genuine Integration of the Spiritual Life and Apostolate." This was a particular favorite of Pope Paul VI.

In the 33rd General Congregation we read: "... we must continually renew our efforts if we are to enter more deeply into the meaning of our lives as Jesuits: men totally committed to the glory of God and the service of others. As a consequence, the general congregation invites all Jesuits to strive, personally and communally, toward an even greater integration of our spiritual life and apostolate" (n.10–11).

When we turn to our ministries and apostolic activity, we find a very frank treatment in the 31st General Congregation. It found that "our labors have not produced all the results that we could rightly expect" and several reasons are cited for this: "failure continually to renew our apostolic or missionary spirit," "failure to maintain the union which the instrument should have with God," and " a too great scattering of our forces." The principal reason, however, is the "failure to adequately adapt our ministries to the changed conditions of our times" (decree 21, n.1). The congregation continued: "We need to be more available to take on those ministries which answer the urgent pastoral needs of the modern Church and the special missions of the Roman Pontiff . . . Renewal and adaptation require a continual revision of the choice and promotion of our ministries . . . " (nn.2, 3).

This concern in 1965 would be faced squarely in the 32nd General Congregation in 1975, and resolved in the 33rd General Congregation in 1983. The special missions of the Roman Pontiff which are referred to are a distinctive note of our way of proceeding and would continue to play an important role in the life of the Society right through the 32nd and 33rd General Congregations.

The 31st General Congregation turns to the seventh part of the Constitutions where Ignatius sets down the great principles for the selection of our ministries: the greater service of God, the more universal good, the more pressing need, the great importance of a future good, and special care of those significant ministries for which we have special talent (*Constitutions* 622).

These norms have a perennial validity, but the congregation notes that they must always be rightly applied to historical circumstances. And this has been done by the decrees of the general congregations and the instructions of the fathers general (decree 21, n.4).

These principles are very general and idealistic. What Ignatius seems to be telling us is not so much how to choose, as what our attitude of mind and heart should be when we must choose. His principles are intended to keep our vision alive and our minds and hearts open.

Father Arrupe gave us an example of using these Igna-tian criteria in a very concrete historical situation in 1980 when he created the Jesuit Refugee Service. He had been struck and shocked by the plight of so many "boat people" and refugees. In his letter of November 14, 1980, to the whole Society, he wrote:

> At the outset I explained that this situation constitutes a challenge to the Society we cannot ignore if we are to remain faithful to St. Ignatius's criteria for our apostolic work and the recent calls of the 31st and 32nd General Congregations. In the Constitutions, St. Ignatius speaks of the greater uni-versal good, an urgency that is ever growing, the difficulty and complexity of the human problem involved, and the lack of other people to attend to the need (*Constitutions* 623). With our ideal of availability and universality, the number of institutions under our care, and the active collaboration of many lay people who work with us, we are particularly well fitted to meet this challenge and provide services that are not being catered to sufficiently by other organizations and groups ... The Society is being called to render a service that is human, pedagogical and spiritual ... I consider this as a new modern apostolate for the Society as a whole, of great importance for today and the future, and of much spiritual benefit also to the Society . . . St. Ignatius called us to go anywhere we are most needed for the greater service of God . . . God is calling us through these helpless people (*Acta Romana* XVIII 1980, pp. 319–21).

This is an excellent example of how our Ignatian spiri-tuality has influenced our ministry. It also shows the use of the *magis,* so dear to Ignatius, in the magnanimity shown in an-swering God's call through his people. There is also a clear sense of compassion as we contemplate the women and men and children of our world as Ignatius suggests in the "Contem-plation on the Incarnation" (*Spiritual Exercises* 102, 106). Mag-nanimity and compassion are a part of our way of proceeding that flows over into our ministries and labors. So, too, is the collaboration with lay people which is clear in Pedro Arrupe's proposal. And finally, there is an involvement which is not purely material but which is "a service that is human, pedagogical and spiritual." This is really a good example of our topic.

The 31st General Congregation issued seventeen decrees on the apostolate in urging the Society to an apostolic renewal (decrees 21–37). As a general method it proposed the constitution of commissions to be set up in the provinces or on an interprovincial basis. In its pastoral services the Society made a significant change in its policy of accepting parishes. Since the discipline of the church in regard to parishes committed to religious had been changed, the Society was now open to accepting parishes.

Of special import to all Jesuit ministries was the mandate given to the Society by Pope Paul VI at the beginning of the 31st General Congregation: "The Supreme Pontiff Paul VI, on the occasion of the gathering of the Fathers for the 31st General Congregation, committed to the Society, in view of its special vow of obedience, the task of resisting atheism 'with forces united.' Each Jesuit, therefore, earnestly though humbly, should take part in this task by prayer and action . . . " (decree 3, n.1). The congregation also indicated that this mandate should permeate all the accepted forms of our apostolate (n.11). This mandate was confirmed by the successors of Paul VI and has become more concrete over the years. Atheism is understood as all forms of unbelief and disbelief. The bond of love and service that binds the Society to the vicar of Christ, as expressed in the Formula of our Institute, is a fundamental element in our way of proceeding.

Thus the 31st General Congregation began a renewal in our apostolic way of life, and it paved the way for the 32nd General Congregation which focused on apostolic renewal.

The 32nd General Congregation lasted from December 2, 1974, to March 7, 1975. The aim was to refocus the apostolic service of the Society in a line of continuity with its original charism, but also in a spirit of adaptation to the changed conditions of the modern world. These changed conditions were such that the Society could no longer settle for its older models of service.

Despite some very trying and difficult moments, the congregation's main accomplishment was to renew and update the apostolic orientation of the Society. Its introductory decree gives a clear and, at times, blunt description of the situation in the Society after the 31st General Congregation. It can be helpful to us with regard to the genuine Ignatian spirit:

> The past decade in the life of the Society has been an effort under the leadership of Father General (Arrupe) to implement the decrees of the 31st General Congregation, which aimed at adapting our life to the directives of the Second Vatican Council. The success of this effort has been significant in our apostolic work as a community, in our prayer and our faith . . . The 32nd General Congregation makes its own and confirms all of the declarations and dispositions of the 31st General Congregation unless they are explicitly changed in the present decrees. The documents of the preceding congregation accurately and faithfully express the genuine spirit and tradition of the Society. Therefore, the whole Society is urged to reflect thoughtfully and sincerely upon those documents once again, and superiors are directed to see to their ever fuller implementation. One reason for this directive is that the progress mentioned above has not been uniform. Some Jesuits have resisted renewal and have even criticized the 31st General Congregation publicly, as though it were somehow a departure from the genuine Ignatian spirit. Others, at times, have carried new orientations to excess in their impatience to accommodate themselves and their work to the needs of the world . . . Mindful that for the majority of Jesuits the years since the 31st General Congregation have been a time of grace and spiritual and apostolic growth, the 32nd General Congregation has formulated these decrees as an invitation to even greater progress in the way of the Lord . . . These decrees, then, are meant for practical implementation. Only the cooperation of all Jesuits under the leadership of their superiors can achieve this goal (decree 1, nn.1–10).

The principal and key decree of the 32nd General Congregation is decree 4: "Our Mission Today: The Service of

Faith and the Promotion of Justice." It defines the mission of the Society today: "The mission of the Society of Jesus today is the service of faith, of which the promotion of justice is an absolute requirement. For reconciliation with God demands the reconciliation of people with one another" (n.2). But this new focus is in continuity with the mission stated in the Formula of the Institute (n.1): "In one form or another, this has always been the mission of the Society; but it gains new meaning and urgency in the light of the needs and aspirations of the men and women of our time, and it is in that light that we examine it anew. We are confronted today, in fact, by a whole series of new challenges" (n.3). This decree is the clearest and most explicit expression of the will of our Society to meet the challenges and expectations of our world today, while remaining faithful to its original charism. It seeks to fulfill what Vatican II had asked of all religious institutes.

The impact of decree 4 was felt in almost all the other decrees of the congregation, and particularly in decree 2, "Jesuits Today" which is a response to requests for a description of Jesuit identity in our time, and in decree 11, "The Union of Minds and Hearts," which gives orientations and guidelines for our spiritual life and our life in community.

This mission of the Society calls for a response that must be total, corporate, rooted in faith and experience, and multiform. Total means that we must put everything into this enterprise, all that we are and have, our whole persons, our communities, institutions, ministries, and resources (decree 4, n.7). Corporate means "each one of us must contribute to the total mission according to his talents and functions which, in collaboration with the efforts of others, give life to the whole body. This collaborative mission is exercised under the leadership of Peter's Successor who presides over the universal church and over all those whom the Spirit of God has appointed Pastors over the churches" (n.7). Rooted in faith and experience means that "it is from faith and experience combined that we will learn how to respond most appropriately to new needs arising from new situations" (n.7). Multiform means that "since these situations are different in different parts of the world, we must cultivate a great adaptability and flexibility within the single, steady aim of the service of faith and the promotion of justice" (n.7).

An extremely important consequence is that "we must undertake a thoroughgoing reassessment of our traditional apostolic methods, attitudes, and institutions with a view to adapting them to the new needs of the times and to a world in process of rapid change" (n.9).

A very special method to be used is that of discernment: "All this demands that we practice discernment, that spiritual discernment which St. Ignatius teaches us in the Exercises" (n.10).

Four areas of the apostolate are singled out because of their importance:

> The General Congregation wishes to continue along the lines given by Father General (Arrupe) to the Congregation of Procurators of 1970, and to emphasize once more the importance of theological reflection, social action, education, and the mass media as means of making our preaching of the Gospel more effective. The importance of these means rests in the fact that, in touching its most profound needs, they permit a more universal service to mankind (n.59).

The ministry of the Spiritual Exercises is one of great importance: "A key element in the pedagogy of the Exercises is that its aim is to remove the barriers between God and Man, so that the Spirit speaks directly with the man. Inherent in this Ignatian practice of spiritual direction is a deep respect for the exercitant as he is and for the culture, background, and tradition that have gone into making him what he is. Moreover, the pedagogy of the Exercises is a pedagogy of discernment" (nn.57–58).

On the practical level, each province or group of provinces must undertake a program of reflection and a review of its apostolates (n.71), and there is to be a constant interplay between experience, reflection, decision, and action in line with the Jesuit ideal of being "contemplative in action" (n.73). There is to be in each province or region a definite mechanism for the review of our ministries (n.77).

Decree 2 of the 32nd General Congregation, entitled

"Jesuits Today," gives an excellent summary of the elements in decree 4. Although it is placed first after the introductory decree, in fact decree 2 was among the last decrees to be finished because the congregation developed it during the discussions on the faith/justice relationship. The conclusion of decree 2 has become part of Ignatian spirituality:

> Thus, whether we consider the needs and aspirations of the men of our time, or reflect on the particular charism that founded our Society, or seek to learn what Jesus has in his heart for each and all of us, we are led to the identical conclusion that today the Jesuit is a man whose mission is to dedicate himself entirely to the service of faith and the promotion of justice, in a communion of life and work and sacrifice with the companions who have rallied round the same standard of the Cross and in fidelity to the Vicar of Christ, for the building up of a world at once more human and more divine (n.31).

Our Ignatian charism and spirituality are mission-centered. The Formula of the Institute in the sixteenth century articulated the mission of the Society, and this same mission has been restated authentically in the last three general congregations as the faith that does justice in the name of the Gospel. This is our mission, and our ministries are the means for pursuing this one, universal mission. This mission must be seen as normative for our decision-making process in choosing our ministries.

From the long and lively experience of the Spiritual Exercises in his own life and in the lives of others, Pedro Arrupe had an intuitive grasp of what is essential to the Ignatian charism. He never lets us forget that the whole vocation of a Jesuit is dominated by his "being sent." This concept of "mission" with its companion idea of "availability" had to become a part of the very lifeblood of a Jesuit, since it is a key to the Spiritual Exercises in which the Society had its beginnings. This is the heart of Jesuit identity. This is the quality that impressed Ignatius as specific to the Son and therefore to the Jesuit who believes in the Son and is called to be conformed to his image in the world of today. Only through this thorough availability can we aspire and live up to the condition of "being sent" which guarantees our present integration and true apostolic identity. Ignatian spirituality is focused on the central objective of forming a person who is available for mission. It is not just an individual availability but of the Society as a whole. We should note that mission is not something extrinsic or merely functional. It is primarily a permanent personal attitude by which a Jesuit presents a total availability to the universal Church, and through which the Society is a body for mission.

The period following the 32nd General Congregation was a difficult one, and the new focusing of our mission on the service of faith and the promotion of justice caused tensions both in the Society and outside it. In numerous talks and writings, Father Arrupe worked to explain the true meaning of our mission today; he worked to overcome readings of decree 4 that he termed "incomplete, slanted, and unbalanced" (Rooted and Grounded in Love, 67 in *Acta Romana* XVIII, 500). Instead of an integration of faith and justice, some were emphasizing one aspect of the decree in a unilateral fashion. The result was a kind of exaggerated social activism, close to a merely secular activism on the one side, and a sort of disincarnate spiritualism on the other. This situation, obviously, had a serious effect on the ministries of the Society and even on the basic question of what the original Ignatian charism meant. To clear the air, Pedro Arrupe wrote one of his most moving addresses in February 1981, Rooted and Grounded in Love. It proved to be a great help in the 33rd General Congregation. This address was written only months before the stroke that incapacitated Father Arrupe, and it is part of his spiritual legacy to the Society.

Father Arrupe is speaking of something which was very close to his heart, and I shall quote at some length:

When the 32nd General Congregation, with its supreme authority, defined in a decree how the *defensio et propagatio fidei* of our Formula is to be translated to apply to the concrete situation of today's world, it was aware that countless men and women everywhere on earth are being denied justice. It therefore interpreted the *defensio et propagatio fidei*—or "being a Jesuit today," which is the same thing—as meaning "to engage, under the standard of the cross, in the crucial struggle of our time: the struggle for faith and that struggle for justice which it includes" (decree 2, n.2). The process by which the Society arrived at that formulation was much like the conversion process of the Exercises and followed the same dynamic of total, loving and distinguished surrender to Christ's cause. The Society acknowledged its past deficiencies in the service of faith and the promotion of justice, and asked itself before Christ crucified out of love, to choose participation in the struggle for faith and justice as the focal point that identifies what Jesuits today are and do.

That decision seemed a great step forward, and the Society has been striving since then to carry it out. We still need perspective to evaluate the current balance of well-meant failures and undeniable successes which that option has produced in the Church through the Society. In the light of the most recent encyclical, *Dives in Misercordia*, we may say that, with all the imperfections of any human choice, it was an option in the right direction. However, this is not sufficient; it is not the last step. The congregation realized that charity is the "final step" and basis of everything, and that true justice starts from and is crowned in charity. "There is no genuine conversion to the love of God without conversion to the love of neighbor and, therefore, to the demands of justice. Hence, fidelity to our apostolic mission requires that we propose the whole of Christian salvation and lead others to embrace it. Christian salvation consists in an undivided love of the Father and of the neighbor and of justice. Since evangelization is proclamation of the faith which is made operative in love of others, the promotion of justice is indispensable to it" (decree 4, n.28). Further on in that same decree 4, the congregation affirmed: "If the promotion of justice is to attain its ultimate end, it should be carried out in such a way as to bring men and women to desire and to welcome the eschatological freedom and salvation offered to us by God in Christ. The methods we employ and the activities we undertake should express the spirit of the Beatitudes and bring people to a real reconciliation" (n.33). We should keep these paragraphs of decree 4 well in mind, so that our reading of it will not be incomplete, slanted, or unbalanced. The Society still has to advance in its understanding of , and search for, that justice which it has pledged itself to promote. I am sure the effort will lead us to discover an even wider field—that of charity.

Yes, justice is not enough. The world needs a stronger cure, a more effective witness, and more effective deeds: those of love . . .

. . . The plight of the world, I can confidently assert, so deeply wounds our sensibilities as Jesuits that it sets the inmost fibres of our apostolic zeal a-tingling. Our historical mission is involved in all this, for the purpose of our Society is the defense and propagation of the faith, and we know that faith moves and is moved by charity, and that charity brings about and goes beyond justice. The struggle for faith, the promotion of justice, the commitment to charity, all these are our objective, and in it lies our raison d'être. Our *accommodata renovatio* consists in letting ourselves be imbued by this idea and in living it with all the intensity of the Ignatian *magis* (nn.66–73).

You are all familiar, I'm sure, with the papal intervention in the government of the Society in 1981 after Father Arrupe's stroke, and in the consequent preparation for the 33rd General Congregation which began on September 2, 1983. Despite the tensions and difficult moments, the congregation was a great moment for the Society as an apostolic body. After honestly admitting certain defects, the congregation confirmed the orientation of the 31st and 32nd General Congregations and set the path for the future. One has to be familiar with the history of events through the two prior general congregations in order to appreciate the following words of the 33rd General Congregation:

In the light, therefore, of requests coming from the whole Society, the needs of the world, and the Church's teaching, the 33rd General Congregation readily receives the calls which the pope has made to the Society, and commits itself to a full and prompt response. At the same time we confirm the Society's mission expressed by the 31st and 32nd General Congregations, particularly in the latter's

decrees 2 and 4, which are the application today of the Formula of the Institute and of our Ignatian charism. They express our mission today in profound terms offering insights that serve as guidelines for our future responses:
    —The integration of the service of faith and promotion of justice in one single mission; (decree 2, n.8)
    —the universality of the mission in the various ministries in which we engage; (decree 2, n.9)
    —the *discernment* needed to implement this mission; (decree 4, n.10)
    —the *corporate* nature of this mission (decree 4, nn.62–69).

The mission, therefore, of the whole Society and of every Jesuit is the integration of the service of faith and the promotion of justice in the name of the Gospel. This mission is not simply one mission among others. It must be the integrating factor of all our ministries. To fulfill this mission, we must be faithful to the practice of personal and corporate discernment. Our communities must be apostolic communities and must have for their principle of unity the apostolic spirit. This is how we remain faithful to our Ignatian charism while adapting our ministries to the changed conditions of our times. This is our way of proceeding.

How do we respond to this mission of the Society, especially with regard to the selection of ministries? The missions that we receive from the Holy Father play a key role in our Ignatian spirituality, in our way of proceeding. The 33rd General Congregation translated into a language proper to our Society the missions which Pope John Paul II, in his own name and in the name of his predecessors, had given to us on two special occasions: the allocution given to the provincial superiors on February 27, 1982, in Rome, and the homily at the concelebrated Mass which opened the 33rd General Congregation on September 2, 1983.

Having considered the challenges of the world we live in, the general congregation declared: "It is in this context that we Jesuits hear the calls that have come to us from recent popes. Their calls give apostolic orientations to our mission today. As we opened the 33rd General Congregation, we heard Pope John

Paul II tell us: 'the Church today expects the Society to contribute effectively to the implementation of the Second Vatican Council.'" The missions which the Holy Father cited are: an urgent call to resist atheism vigorously in all its forms of unbelief and false belief; cooperation in the profound renewal needed by the Church in a secularized world; adapting and renewing so many forms of traditional apostolates according to the different spiritual needs of today (e.g., the renewal of Christian life, the education of youth, the formation of the clergy, the study of philosophy and theology, research into humanistic and scientific cultures, and missionary activity); the effort to pursue the apostolic initiatives of Vatican II (ecumenism, the Church's dialogue with non-Christian religions and with different cultures); the integration into the Church's evangelizing activity of inculturation, and of action for the promotion of justice and peace (n.37).

That represents a formidable array of activities, and any Provincial would be delighted to have the men to cover them. We must remember that the Pope was thinking in terms of our international Society all over the world.

The congregation made some applications to help us in responding to our mission. It noted that "traditional apostolates take on fresh importance, while new needs and situations make new demands of us. The essential ministries of preaching the Gospel, fostering sacramental life, giving the Exercises, teaching, formation of the clergy, the work of catechetics, the promotion of Christian communities, and evangelizing those who have not yet heard of Christ—all should contribute to strengthening the faith that does justice" (n.43).

"Of great importance," the congregation continued,

> among the ministries of the Society are the educational and intellectual apostolates...Research in theology and philosophy, in the other sciences, and in every branch of human culture is likewise essential if Jesuits are to help the Church understand the contemporary world and speak to it the Word of Salvation...Jesuits in these fields and our men in more direct social and pastoral ministries should cooperate and benefit from one another's expertise and experience.

Finally, the Society should promote the apostolate of the social communications media which, like education and intellectual work, reaches large numbers of people and so permits a more universal service to humankind (n.44).

The congregation sums up our way of proceeding in working to fulfill our mission in this way:

> If we are to fulfill our mission, we must be faithful to that practice of communal apostolic discernment so central to "our way of proceeding," a practice rooted in the Exercises and Constitutions. This way of proceeding calls for a review of all our ministries, both traditional and new. Such a review includes: an attentiveness to the Word of God; an examen and reflection inspired by the Ignatian tradition; a personal and communitarian conversion necessary in order to become "contemplatives in action"; an effort to live in indifference and availability that will enable us to find God in all things; and a transformation of our habitual patterns of thought through a constant interplay of experience, reflection, and action. We must also always apply those criteria for action found in the seventh part of the Constitutions as well as recent and more specific instructions concerning choice of ministries (GC 31, d. 21–32; GC 32, d. 4, n.60) and occupations or tasks to be avoided (GC 32, d. 4, n.80). This process, undertaken in the local community, province, or region, leads to apostolic decisions made by superiors, after normal consultation and with accountability to Father General (nn.39–40).

The authenticity in our apostolic way of proceeding has to be verified constantly in our Society. One test for this is apostolic discernment which is the only way to work in constant fidelity to the voice of the Spirit in and for his Church. The other test is poverty. The general congregation did not enter into concrete details of an authentic life of apostolic poverty, but it gave a new impetus in applying to the lives of all Jesuits and to every Jesuit ministry the preferential option for the poor. "This option is a decision," the congregation explained, "to love the poor preferentially because there is a desire to heal the whole human family. Such love, like Christ's own, excludes no one, but neither does it excuse anyone from its demands. Directly or indirectly this option should find some concrete expression in every Jesuit's life, in the orientation of our existing apostolic works, and in our choice of new ministries" (n. 48).

This step forward in witnessing to apostolic poverty is at the same time a return to our basic source, the Spiritual Exercises. The Exercises consider it to be "always better and more secure in what touches one's person and condition of life to be more sparing and to cut back and to come nearer to our High Priest, our model and rule, who is Christ our Lord" in His way of serving the Faith and the poor (*Spiritual Exercises*, 344).

Father Peter-Hans Kolvenbach, S.J., our superior general, has spoken very frankly of the difficulty of our mission. "Without doubt," he says,

> all the tasks which the Church entrusts to us entail risks in their accomplishment. To announce to a world distant from the Church the love of God manifested in Jesus Christ; to do this by means of social commitment and inculturation, dialogue and ecumenism, theological research and pastoral experience—this requires of us initiatives which lay us open to misunderstanding. Let us recognize in this fact still another reason why we must continually center in the apostolic body of the Society itself our mission to be men in the front lines, and another reason for making it clear within the Church itself that we are living out an authentic mission within the Church, a mission given by the Church. This "missionary" openness to a world at a distance from the Church or allergic to the Church will not always be understood by those ecclesiastical movements whose apostolic priority is primarily or exclusively the reinforcement of ecclesiastical structures or the unification of the faithful alone. Fortunately we are encouraged by the fact that His Holiness John Paul II affirmed and confirmed these specific missions of the Society's apostolate at the opening of the 33rd General Congregation ("The Society's Reception of the 33rd General Congregation," a letter of Fr. Kolvenbach to the whole Society, March 3, 1985, n.24).

The 32nd General Congregation experienced many moments of tension and difficulty, but one of its electric moments took place on December 20, 1974, when Father Arrupe spoke. It was still a long time before the congregation approved decree 4 on the Society's mission as the service of faith and the promotion of justice. He stated that the justice of the Gospel should be preached through the cross and from the cross and often with the accompaniment of pain and suffering.

> Is our General Congregation ready to take up this responsibility and to carry it out to its ultimate consequences? Is it ready to enter upon the more severe way of the cross, which surely will mean for us a lack of understanding on the part of civil and ecclesiastical authority and of our best friends? Does the General Congregation find itself disposed to offer true witness in its life, works, and ways of acting? Is it prepared to give testimony not just by a decree or declaration that expresses in words the sense or manner of thinking of all or of the greater part of the Congregation, but by reducing that testimony to practice by means of concrete decisions which ought necessarily to change our way of living and working, our field of activity, the social level of those with whom we deal, even our very image and social esteem? . . . The Society of Jesus, as such, should directly assume this initiative of which we speak; it should inspire its sons so that they will give themselves entirely to this apostolate; it should sustain them in difficulties, and even defend them when they are subjected to unjust persecutions arising from this or that source . . . In this "decisive hour" our response will be the concrete expression of that "more precious and more important oblation" that we have so often made in the Exercises (Pedro Arrupe, *Justice with Faith Today*, pp. 205–206).

Less than three years later on March 19, 1977, he addressed a letter to the whole Society on "Paying the Price of the GC 32 Commitment: Our Recent Five Third World Martyrs." Five Jesuits had been murdered, one in El Salvador, one in Brazil, and three in Zimbabwe. In his letter Father Arrupe said:

> The Lord speaks to the Society through the pouring out of their blood. Mingled with our deep grief . . . is a great happiness, unmistakable proof that through these deaths Jesus

Christ has a message for the Society. Who are the victims God has chosen? The five were men of average human gifts, leading obscure lives, more or less unrecognized, dwelling in small villages and totally dedicated to the daily service of the poor and suffering . . . Their style of life was simple, austere, evangelical: it was a life that used them up slowly, day-by-day, in the service of "the little ones." Why did the Lord choose them? I believe it is precisely because of their evangelical life, one that is clearly apostolic and in which the image of a true "companion of Jesus" is never blurred. They were, therefore, unquestionably following the lines of action that the 32nd General Congregation marked out for the Society: the service of faith and the promotion of justice. The Lord seems once again to be showing us his preferences and to be pointing out the values and the kind of witness that he holds in great esteem . . . If we follow Christ, persecution will come, as we have discovered through experience in so many countries when we try to serve faith and promote justice. Not all of us will witness to Christ by shedding our life's blood in sacrifice, but all of us should unreservedly offer him our whole lives. To be able to carry out this vocation of ours, the Society today must count on men and communities imbued with the "mind of Christ," who serve Christ without limit or reservation, who joyfully live lives of evangelical simplicity and continuing self-sacrifice, thus offering to modern man an ideal for living and to the generous youth of our day a model and way of life . . . This is the Jesuit that St. Ignatius, that the Pope, and above all that the eternal King wishes today to find in each one of us (ibid., pp. 206–208).

When Pedro Arrupe spoke to the Congregation of Procurators in 1978, the list of martyrs had grown to eleven. The general congregation in 1983 noted that "our service of faith and promotion of justice has made the Society confront the mystery of the Cross: some Jesuits have been exiled, imprisoned, or put to death in their work of evangelization" (n.31). The list of Jesuits killed numbers thirty-three today. They were killed in Chad, Brazil, six in Zimbabwe, El Salvador, Guyana, India, Bolivia, the Philippines, Guatemala, China, Lebanon, and Mozambique.

Persecutions in the eyes of Ignatius are a sign of fidelity

to Christ, a sign that we are not of this world. Ignatius's own life taught him experientially that the following of Christ brings much hostility.

That is how we understand the conclusion of the 33rd General Congregation: "In the task of announcing the Gospel, faith in Jesus Christ is first and last. It is a faith which comes alive only in works of love and justice" (n.50).

The Society is seen as a body "for mission," a body to be sent, a single body with many members and functions, but having communion in the one Lord alone, and in one total mission. This body is a community of discernment and of humble service; one, moreover, that is open to collaborate disinterestedly with all men and women of good will who seek the Kingdom and spend themselves in order to achieve it.

The whole apostolic body of the Society is called to engage in apostolic discernment, whether that be at the general, the provincial, or the local level of government. This apostolic discernment is a reflection in the context of prayer on the human reality actually at hand. This reality is to be examined as clearly and objectively as possible, and also in the light of faith in the Spirit and in the Church. This is to enable us to establish, in accord with the unchanging apostolic demands of our Ignatian charism, the future orientation to which the Spirit calls us in and for the Church. These orientations are translated into choices among desirable apostolic activities, and decisions to renew or to close or to open apostolic works. And thus, by means of prayer and communal discernment, vision and apostolic government, we undergo a gradual assimilation of the apostolic pedagogy of Ignatius. In this way we overcome our habitual way of absolutizing our perceptions and actions.

Jesuits are men of the Church, and our mission is an ecclesial one. From Ignatius to Peter-Hans Kolvenbach, the Society has considered fidelity to the vicar of Christ as so fundamental to our charism that it is a condition of the very existence of the Society. The situation of the Church in the wake of Vatican II is such that we cannot simply turn to Ignatius's Rules for Thinking with the Church (*Spiritual Exercises*, 352ff.) for immediate solutions to the ecclesial problems of today. We have to learn how to live and act in situations of confrontation and injustice, of misunderstanding and conflict, and of public dissent. We have to learn in, with, and for the Church how to live and proclaim the Gospel in the conditions, cultures, and languages of our time. Our effort must be to build up the Church by proclaiming the mystery of the Church in such a way that people will be able to find in it the face of Christ, the dwelling place of the Spirit, and the house of the Father. We have to learn to grow in what Ignatius called "the true sense which should be ours in the Church." This is a Church with great ecumenical sensitivity, a keen sense of religious liberty and of dialogue, deep concern to defend the rights of God and human rights, and a sense of shared responsibility in building up the Lord's Church. Our culture is quick to denounce publicly all forms of discrimination or injustice, regardless of its source.

Ignatius' Rules for Thinking with the Church do indicate a general way of acting: it is always situated in the movement of the Spirit which directs the Spiritual Exercises and which is always a Spirit of love. This way of acting is centered on the Ignatian concern "to help souls," i.e., on the pastoral care not to weaken or disorientate the people of God and add to divisions and polarizations, but rather to build up the Church vigorously and creatively. This can mean deepening faith through teaching and theological research. The greater service can be that of theological and scientific competence. Our way of acting should make us live, feel, and suffer the Church's problems and limitations as our own, offering with the freedom and humility of the sons of God the charitable service of a constructive criticism that is, in effect, a self-criticism.

Living the authentic Ignatian charism will ensure an apostolic and missionary dynamism in our lives and works. Our way of proceeding resounds in the farewell address of Pedro Arrupe to the Society on September 3, 1983:

> ... In these eighteen years my one ideal was to serve the Lord and his Church—with all my heart—from the beginning to end. I thank the Lord for the great progress which I have witnessed in the Society. Obviously, there would be defects, too—my own, to begin with—but it remains a fact that there was great progress, in personal conversion, in the

apostolate, in concern for the poor, for refugees. And special mention must be made of the attitude of loyalty and filial obedience shown toward the Church and the Holy Father, particularly in these last years. For all of this, thanks be to God . . . My call to you today is that you be available to the Lord. Let us put God at the center, ever attentive to his voice, ever asking what we can do for his more effective service, and doing it to the best of our ability, with love and perfect detachment. Let us cultivate a very personal awareness of the reality of God . . . I am full of hope, seeing the Society at the service of the one Lord and of the Church, under the Roman Pontiff, the vicar of Christ on earth. May she keep going along this path, and may God bless us with many good vocations of priests and brothers: for this I offer to the Lord what is left of my life, my prayers and the sufferings imposed by my ailments. For myself, all I want is to repeat from the depths of my heart; "take Lord, and receive all my liberty, my memory, my understanding and my entire will—all that I have and possess. You have given it all to me. To you, Lord, I return it. All is yours; do with it what you will. Give me only your love and your grace. That is enough for me."

Vincent T. O'Keefe, S.J.
Jesuit Conference
Washington, D.C.

A Response to Vincent O'Keefe, S.J.

Wilton D. Gregory, D.S.L.

Given the wealth of nearly six years of "episcopal wisdom" to call upon, I have begun to understand with a little more accuracy why certain invitations cross my desk. The requests generally fall into several easily identifiable categories. The first would be, "He might relate better to our young people, since he may even remember being a young person himself!" Then, "We hear he has some facility in liturgy." And finally, "We are looking for some 'African-American presence,' and he's the best we could come up with!" These are not bad reasons; as a matter of fact, they are quite understandable and perhaps even noble! Yet they proved to be completely insufficient in helping me to understand why I received this wonderful request to share in your Charism Days. I could not fathom the invitation to share in these Ignatian Charism Days other than perhaps a one last-ditch attempt on the part of some of my erstwhile Jesuit professors to redeem themselves in the eyes of their colleagues—hoping, of course, that I might offer some insight that was of modest significance! Whatever the reasons for your kind invitation, I am flattered and pleased to share these observations with you. Since accepting your invitation almost a year ago, I now have personal reasons to take this opportunity to express my gratitude to the Chicago Province of the Society of Jesus for accepting the pastoral care of Our Lady of the Gardens parish in Altgeld Gardens in my vicariate. I look forward to working more closely with you in the mutual service to the people of this far Southside parish.

Although you have spent this past year exploring the foundations of your charisms as Jesuits, and this in open dialogue with the contemporary demands of the Church, Vincent O'Keefe's address extended this dialogue to include a process which was set in motion by the three most recent general congregations, beginning with the 31st which elected Pedro Arrupe superior general in 1965. The 31st, 32nd, and 33rd General Congregations have all been reflective moments for the Society of Jesus in assisting you in the task of translating your charism as Jesuits into the language that the world speaks today to express its pastoral and spiritual needs and hungers. May I highlight six points raised by Vincent's presentation and address them as one who is simultaneously a bishop, without benefit of being a priest from a religious community; an African-American native of Chicago; and one who has enjoyed the personal friendship of a number of Jesuits both here in Chicago and in Rome.

It seems to me that it is impossible for a Jesuit to understand where he is needed in the world today in isolation. Even fortified with the resources of the Ignatian spiritual patrimony, weighty to be sure, there is still a need to listen to the needs of the contemporary Church as it invites the Society of Jesus to accept, as did Ignatius himself, the challenge to work for the greater glory of God in quite specific contexts. Here a local bishop has to temper the pressures he may feel to respond to the growing pastoral needs of a particular church in respect to the religious charisms of the Society of Jesus. In short, we need one another. Perhaps the Lord speaks to both the local bishop and to the Society in this time of the diminishing numbers of ordained ministers to discover which, if any, of the pastoral needs of a diocese can best and most appropriately be satisfied through the generous service of the Society of Jesus. Moreover, Jesuits should not be asked to assume just any pastoral position in a local church simply because there is an opening that has not been satisfied through other resources.

We bishops must come to understand, through open

and fraternal dialogue, how the Society envisions its service in a local setting. A bishop might need a priest; but there is a second and equally important question to be raised, would a Jesuit priest be the best person in this particular pastoral service. This means that bishops and the Society of Jesus must be in honest and open dialogue about the charisms of the Society and the needs of the diocese. In particular, Vincent reminded us that the 31st General Congregation referred to the 7th Part of the Constitutions where Ignatius himself established the principle for selecting a ministry which exhibited "the more pressing need." Surely that means significantly more than simply "a hard-to-fill assignment." It speaks of a ministry which is a Gospel challenge and not simply less clerically desirable for whatever reason. Here it seems that service to the poor would most conveniently fit the category of "a more pressing need." Poverty, of course, takes many forms, but spiritual and economic empoverishment enjoy first place in the Church's understanding of the term. Thus bishops who are privileged to work with the Society of Jesus ought to know their dioceses and the Society of Jesus well enough to be able to invite the Jesuits to fulfill this Ignatian directive of service within the local church. And the Jesuit principle of accepting a ministry according to "more pressing need" might well aid the bishop himself in viewing a pastoral need.

Second, the principal and key decree of the 32nd General Congregation is "the service of faith and the promotion of justice." In an analogous way to the interrelatedness of sacred scripture and sacred tradition in the Church's understanding of divine revelation (*Dei verbum*, Art. 10), the service of faith and the promotion of justice are not disjunct, nor are they temporally at odds with one another. It is impossible to promote justice and not simultaneously serve the faith, and vice versa. In a city like Chicago, it is unthinkable that the Catholic Church could find itself in the position of injustice and not also at the same time be in heresy.

Third, among the four areas of the apostolate singled out by Pedro Arrupe in 1970, the fourth, mass media, is in great need of attention. I believe that our Church needs significant assistance in making more effective use of mass media. Quite simply, we are not reaching our people with the message of the Gospel because, for the most part, we are using means that no longer are considered to be the most effective. Long pastoral letters and lengthier homilies and speeches are not the means to touch our people. The electronic media, the printed media, and the media employed by advertising reach more people with counter-Gospel values than we can even imagine. The Catholic press has been divided into the ideological camps of the extreme right and the extreme left, and the middle has been left uninformed and disinterested! If the Society of Jesus could offer a significant insight into how to make better use of the mass media, a future generation of Catholics would hold you in even higher regard!

Fourth, you Jesuits must view your mission in the world as a common charism. Even though you engage in a variety of apostolic activities, there must be a oneness that is apparent to all whom you serve. There are no first class or second class Jesuits, professional or labor Jesuits, pastoral or academic Jesuits. There is only the presence in the Church of a community of men whose mission is the service of the faith and the promotion of justice, although this is accomplished in quite different ways and manners.

Fifth, one of the crosses that I have come to accept as a bishop is "the poverty of being misunderstood." I do not think of myself as a person with masochistic leanings. I always envisioned myself before my third heady anointing with chrism—perhaps with delusion—as being fairly popular with family, friends, and colleagues. Never have I understood more deeply the rich wisdom of John when he cautions us: "No need, then, brothers, to be surprised if the world hates you" (1 John 3:13). Yet we continue to be surprised in spite of countless Gospel references to the hatred and mistreatment that being Jesus' disciples brings. It is a poverty to be misunderstood, publicly criticized and ridiculed, unfairly accused of being either heretical or Neanderthal! I do not suppose that I shall ever grow accustomed to being misunderstood—it would be a sign of emotional unbalance to do so. But the development of a willingness to accept misunderstanding as a sign and an expression of the poverty we embrace when we embrace Christ Jesus gives more meaning to poverty than I had ever envisioned before hearing of it through the wisdom of Pedro Arrupe.

Finally, I commend your desire to engage more directly in the great work of inculturation, which is both the constant mission of the Church and perhaps the most specific challenge of the Second Vatican Council. Inculturation is really the continuation of the Incarnation. The Society of Jesus must see itself being refashioned here in our Chicago community through the more active recruitment of Hispanic, Asian, Black, and Native American candidates. You have a rich tradition of serving young people in your academic institutions, your missionary efforts are extensive, your pastoral service is noteworthy. These encounters with God's people must also change you even as you work to change the lives of those you serve. The small parish of Our Lady of the Gardens last year gave the Church in the United States the first set of twin African-American Catholic priests in the young Smith brothers. Surely there are others, if not there, then among the thousands of young people who look to you for education, good example, pastoral care, and friendship. Somewhere along the way they all ask the disciples' question, "Rabbi, where do you live?" Bring them home into the Society and then invite them into your fraternity!

Wilton D. Gregory, D.S.L.
Auxiliary Bishop of Chicago

A Response to Vincent O'Keefe, S.J.

Carol Frances Jegen, B.V.M.

Let me begin with a slight variation of the *magis*, the "more" of Saint Ignatius. More than anything else, I hope my remarks today will be an expression of gratitude to you, the Chicago Province Jesuits. You have served my immediate family for six generations, practically from the earliest days of your ministry in this city. You have served my BVM family in countless ways since those Holy Family days when Father Damen brought us to Chicago. Father Damen first met BVMs on one of his mission ventures in eastern Iowa. A sentence or two from an 1867 letter written by Father Laurent, then pastor in Muscatine, Iowa, is particularly significant for our gathering this morning.

> I am confident that their being called to Chicago is the beginning of a new era for them. They will not depend any more on only one diocese and upon the whims and caprice of a few priests, but they will have the Jesuits to guide them, which is saying a great deal.[1]

So now, in gratitude let me respond.

---

[1]As quoted in M. Jane Coogan, BVM, *The Price of Our Heritage,* Mount Carmel Press, Dubuque, Iowa, 1975, p.379.

Father O'Keefe has gifted us with a remarkable synthesis of the last three general congregations. He has focused our hearts on minds andthe central all-pervading truth that Jesuit spirituality always has been, is now, and always will be your resource for ministry. Drawing on the wisdom of Pedro Arrupe, Vincent O'Keefe has reminded us that Jesuit spirituality, the Jesuit way of living attuned to the Spirit of Jesus, has its own particular challenges in this Vatican II era in the life of the Church, our time of New Pentecost.

At this point in your history, perhaps the principal and key decree of the 32nd General Congregation, decree 4, can be considered your climactic renewal statement, resulting from the personal and communal discernment characteristic of your "way of proceeding." With great clarity and precision, decree 4 states: "The mission of the Society of Jesus today is the service of faith, of which the promotion of justice is an absolute requirement. For reconciliation with God demands the reconciliation of people with one another" (n.2). Father O'Keefe's comments on decree 4 call for careful pondering: "This decree is the clearest and most explicit expression of the will of our Society to meet the challenges and expectations of our world today, while remaining faithful to its original charism. It seeks to fulfill what Vatican II had asked of all religious institutes."

You may recall with me that preparations for the 32nd Congregation included a special preparatory meeting at the University of San Francisco in 1973. Representatives from several communities of women religious were invited to participate in that communal discernment process. As one of the BVMs present, I was asked to respond to the paper on obedience. On the final day of the meeting, the feast of Saint Ignatius, several of us found ourselves at dawn celebrating the Eucharist in the San Joaquin Valley. We had traveled through the night, responding to an immediate cry of the poor, in this case, the farmworkers struggling for justice against unbelievable odds and brutal violence. Before that morning was over, many of us had been arrested with the farmworkers and began a two-week incarceration, because we had broken an unjust injunction as we joined the farmworkers on their picket lines. That day, faith that does justice had brought all of us into the mystery of the cross with amazing rapidity. As I look back on that grace-filled experience of preparation for the 32nd General Congregation, I often recall that the farmworker who drove several of us, Jesuits and BVMs, from the celebration of the Eucharist to the picket line was named Jesús. One didn't have to be totally adept at contemplation in action to recognize in that situation that Jesus was leading us into new ways of availability and flexibility in the service of his kingdom.

This morning we have been reminded once again that the struggle for justice must be "rooted and grounded in love," if the justice we are striving for is truly an expression of faith. Can we not say that the relation of justice to charity is already stated in decree 4 in its emphasis on reconciliation? There, the faith that does justice is integrally related to reconciliation. Let us listen to those powerful words once again. "The mission of the Society of Jesus today is the service of faith, of which the promotion of justice is an absolute requirement. For reconciliation with God demands the reconciliation of people with one another." Perhaps the *magis*, the "more" of your apostolic efforts for justice must be seen more and more clearly in the light of reconciliation. And is not the call to reconciliation another way to highlight the Gospel call to peacemaking?

Since the Second Vatican Council the Church has become more aware of the integral relation between justice and peace. The history of the Council's deliberations marks the developing awareness of this essential relationship. In the beginning discussions concerning the formation of a new Pontifical Commission, the thrust was that of *justice*, largely because of the horrendous situation of world hunger. As those discussions continued, the Council Fathers saw the wisdom of widening the thrust to include peace. Consequently, Vatican II eventually gave us the new Pontifical Commission for Justice and Peace.

Pope Paul VI has given us that powerful statement, "If you want peace, work for justice." John Paul II, at the opening of the 33rd General Congregation, reminded you that "the Church today expects the Society to contribute effectively to the implementation of the Second Vatican Council." One of the missions he recalled for you that day was "the integration into the Church's evangelizing activity, of inculturation and of action for the promotion of justice and peace."

Recently, at an international, ecumenical seminar entitled Toward a Theology of Peace, held in Budapest, I met four of your Jesuits who had come from Asia, Latin America, and the United States. One of them, Father Luis Perez Aguirre from Uruguay, had already suffered imprisonment and torture because of his work with abandoned children. I did not need to see the scars of torture, which his sleeves covered, to know that I was speaking with a person strong with the love of a martyr. His face told me that. In an unforgettable way, both in our private conversations and in his prepared address, Fr. Luis witnessed to the unbreakable link between justice and peace. Let me share just a few of his words with you.

> Our major objective, yours and mine, is the stopping of the escalation of nuclear weapons and the feeding of the world's hungry who starve because vital resources are diverted to militarism and the arms race.
>
> But we may discover a significant difference. Your urgent task is to prevent a *possible genocide* in the First World; my urgent task is to halt the *actual genocide* in the Third World.
>
> Today, by midnight, as each day, in the sight of our frightened eyes, more than 45,000 of our children will be dead... because of malnutrition and starvation, and for each child dead, more than 245,000 will continue to live in precarious conditions for the rest of their lives, marked in their minds and bodies by illness. Our poor countries are victims of the violence of the debt crisis. $2 million per minute is paid out in interest on a total world debt of $20 trillion, even more than the $1.5 million per minute spent on militarism. And at the same time almost each second a child is dying of hunger.[2]

You and I are not in Uruguay. We are in Chicago. But more than ever before on the face of our threatened earth, we know that our attitudes and actions have global repercussions. We

---

[2]Luis Perez Aguirre, "Towards a Theology of Peace through the Power of the Poor," in *Toward a Theology of Peace*, Raday College, Budapest, 1987, p.57.

must in all honesty ask how the orientation toward justice and charity, toward reconciliation and peacemaking has permeated our ministries, each and every one of them: your universities, Loyola University Press, your parishes, your high schools, retreat houses, and the many other ministries in which you are involved. All of us who know and love you pray that your discernment will be totally honest and courageous as you face this question.

In closing, I would like to share a little story of my first challenge to Ignatian spirituality. In our elementary school we were encouraged to write AMDG on the top or our papers. We learned what the letters stood for and that this prayer was a favorite one of Saint Ignatius, a very great and important saint. Along about fifth grade, we were studying positive, comparative, and superlative degrees in English grammar. One day I raised my hand and asked our fifth grade Sister, if Saint Ignatius was such a great saint, why would he settle for the *greater* glory of God and not for the *greatest* glory of God.

Only years later, did I really come to understand the wonder and beauty of God's love in leaving the *magis*, the "more" to our free response. My prayer for you today and always is that you are faithful to your *magis*, the "more" of justice which is the charity of reconciliation and peace.

Carol Frances Jegen, B.V.M.
Mundelein College
Chicago, Illinois